One
Anothering

One Anothering

praying through challenges together

Dan R. Crawford & Al Meredith

COVENANT
PUBLISHING

www.covenantpublishing.com

Covenant Publishing
P.O. Box 390, Webb City, Missouri 64870
Call toll free at 877.673.1015

Library of Congress Cataloging-in-Publication Data
Crawford, Dan R., 1941-
   One anothering : praying through challenges together / Dan R. Crawford & Al Meredith.
     p. cm.
   ISBN 1-892435-89-6 (pbk.)
   1. Fellowship—Religious aspects—Baptists—Meditations. 2. Baptists—Prayer-books and devotions—English. 3. Wedgwood Baptist Church (Fort Worth, Tex.) 4. Fellowship—Biblical teaching. I. Meredith, Albert, 1946- II. Title.
   BV4517.5.C73 2004
   286'.17645315—dc22

                              2004017117

In appreciation of and respect for the people of Wedgwood Baptist Church in Fort Worth, Texas, all royalties paid from the sale of this book will be donated to mission-related activities involving members of Wedgwood.

dedicated to
The members of Wedgwood Baptist Church,
Fort Worth, Texas,
who, in the aftermath of a
tragic shooting in the church,
learned how to pray for
one another more effectively.

JR Crawford
Rom 12:5

The unique slant of this book is to give guidance to believers in praying for one another by using the other "one another" passages as directives.

Surely our intercessions for one another clarify God's fame among the unbelieving and confirm God's love for us.

"ONE ANOTHERING"
From a Night of Tragedy to the Dawning of a New Day

How do you make it through a night of tragedy toward the dawning of a new day? A lone gunman carrying two guns, two hundred rounds of ammunition, and a pipe bomb entered the Wedgwood Baptist Church in Fort Worth, Texas, during Wednesday evening activities. In the next twelve minutes, seven people lost their lives, seven others were seriously injured, and hundreds were traumatized.

As the fifth anniversary of the event approached, we were repeatedly asked, "How have the church and its members individually fared since the shooting tragedy?" Even though many still bear the scars and wounds of that night, every measurable category in the church increased, some numbers even doubling and tripling. The spirit and the fellowship have been genuinely enhanced. Missions giving and involvement have shown large increases. Other churches have been started out of Wedgwood's membership. While all the glory correctly goes to God, the survival and growth of the church was aided by Wedgwood's emphasis on prayer.

Thus prayer is among the answers to the questions of how our church survived and thrived. Not just other persons praying for Wedgwood, as thousands from all over the world did on that night and in the days following, but Wedgwood members praying for one another over the last five years. This one-another praying was enhanced by a Wednesday evening Bible study series on the one-another passages in the New Testament.

Now, five years after the event, comes this book on the subject of praying for one another, especially through the challenges of life.

THE GOOD SENSE GOD GAVE A GOOSE

Have you heard the goose lesson? It is a perfect illustration of "one anothering." Geese flying south for the winter usually fly in a V-formation. This formation adds at least seventy-one percent greater flying range, because the flapping of one bird's wings creates uplift for the bird immediately following. When the lead goose gets tired, it rotates back into the flock, and another goose flies point. Geese honk from behind to encourage the lead goose. If a goose gets sick or injured and falls out, two geese follow it down to help protect it. They stay until the fallen goose is able to fly or is dead, and then they join another formation and continue their journey. Should a goose fall out of formation, it quickly feels the difficulty of flying alone and returns immediately to the formation. From childhood, we remember the phrase "the good sense God gave a goose." Sometimes it seems geese possess more God-given sense of "one anothering" than humans do. Fortunately, we have biblical instructions to assist us.

The New Testament has a unique word for this idea. The Greek word *allelon* is translated "one another." Appearing occasionally in the Gospels, the word then appears fifty-eight times in the remainder of the New Testament, with forty of these occurrences found in Paul's letters.

NEW TESTAMENT USES OF THE GREEK WORD ALLELON

■ Mark 9:50—*Be at peace with one another*
■ John 13:14—*Wash one another's feet*
■ John 13:34-35; John 15:12, 17; Romans 13:8; Galatians 5:13; 1 Thessalonians 3:12, 4:9; 1 Peter 1:22; 1 John 3:11, 23; 4:7, 11-12; 2 John 5—*Love one another*
■ Romans 12:5—*Be members of one another*
■ Romans 12:10—*Be devoted to one another*
■ Romans 12:10—*Honor one another*
■ Romans 14:13—*Let us not judge one another*
■ Romans 15:5—*Be of the same mind with one another*
■ Romans 15:7—*Receive one another*
■ Romans 15:14—*Admonish one another*
■ Romans 16:16; 1 Corinthians 16:20; 1 Peter 5:14—*Greet one another*
■ 1 Corinthians 11:33—*Wait for one another*
■ 1 Corinthians 12:25—*Care for one another*
■ Galatians 5:13—*Serve one another*
■ Galatians 5:15—*Do not bite and devour lest you consume one another*
■ Galatians 5:26—*Do not provoke one another*
■ Galatians 5:26—*Do not envy one another*
■ Galatians 6:2—*Bear one another's burdens*
■ Ephesians 4:2; Colossians 3:13—*Bear with one another*
■ Ephesians 4:32—*Be kind to one another*
■ Ephesians 5:21; 1 Peter 5:5—*Submit to one another*
■ Colossians 3:9—*Do not lie to one another*
■ 1 Thessalonians 4:18—*Comfort one another*
■ 1 Thessalonians 5:11—*Edify one another*
■ Hebrews 10:24—*Consider one another*
■ James 4:11—*Do not speak evil of one another*
■ James 5:9—*Do not grumble against one another*
■ James 5:16—*Confess to one another*
■ James 5:16—*Pray for one another*
■ 1 Peter 4:9—*Be hospitable to one another*
■ 1 John 1:7—*Fellowship with one another*

On one occasion, James uses this Greek word when he writes, "Pray for one another" (Jas. 5:16). In the midst of studying the "one another" occurrences in the New Testament, it became apparent that we need much help in fulfilling this prayer encouragement. We know how to pray for ourselves, our families, the world, the nation, all the missionaries, and our churches in general, but how do we pray specifically for one another?

Several good books have been written on the "one another" passages. While some were helpful in this study, the unique slant of this book is to give guidance to believers in praying for one another by using the other "one another" passages as directives.

ANOTHER WORD FOR "ONE ANOTHERING"

The word "intercession' literally means the act of making a request or even pleading on behalf of another or others. It means to intervene for the purpose of producing agreement. It is the role of one who mediates. When used in relation to prayer, it means to pray for another or others. It is a prayer word for "one anothering."

While many prayers in the Bible are offered on behalf of the one praying, the majority of prayers are those offered for others. Southern Baptist prayer leader T.W. Hunt shares from his research that of the prayers in the Bible where an answer is known, seven-ninths (or 78%) are prayers of intercession.

Early in the biblical record (Gen. 18:16-33), God shares with Abraham a plan to destroy the sinful city of Sodom. Faithful intercessor that he was, Abraham pleads with God, appealing to God's righteousness rather than God's mercy, to spare Sodom if fifty faithful men can be found. The prayer produces agreement from God. Abraham persists, asking for the same withholding of destruction if forty-five men can be found, then forty, then thirty, then twenty, then ten. Each time, God agrees. What an Old Testament model for New Testament persistent intercession for one another.

The prince of Old Testament intercessors was Moses. On the occasion of national rebellion and God's promise to "strike them with the pestilence and disinherit them" (Num. 14:12), Moses pleads with God to spare the people. Whereas Abraham had based his intercession on God's righteousness, Moses bases his on the integrity of God's fame among the enemy and the abundance of God's love for the people. Surely our intercessions for one another clarify God's fame among the unbelieving and confirm God's love for us.

The prophet Samuel excelled as an intercessor. After all, he was the son of a praying mother and the student of a praying teacher. The early chapters of 1 Samuel reveal a man who was faithful in interceding for his people. Samuel takes intercession to a new level by indicating that failing to intercede would be a sin. In 1 Samuel 12:23 he says, "Far be it from me that I should sin against the Lord in ceasing to pray for you." So often is the "one anothering" concept mentioned in the New Testament that with Samuel of the Old Testament we may well conclude, failing to pray for one another is a sin against the Lord.

The long climb up prayer mountain reaches a peak in John 17 with what has commonly been called "The High Priestly Prayer of Jesus." Having foretold his death and resurrection and promised his faithfulness in prayer, Jesus "lifted his eyes to heaven" (John 17:1) and began to intercede. Jesus prays first for his disciples, "the men whom You have given me out of the world," and second for new believers who would come into the Kingdom as a result of the ministry of the disciples, "those who will believe in Me through their word." He gives us an ongoing model of one-anothering prayer, since this type of praying by Jesus has not ceased, rather, "He ever lives to make intercession" (Heb. 7:25).

Paul was the great interpreter of Jesus to the Gentile world. In Ephesians 3:14-21, there is found a supreme model for intercession. Here Paul offers what one scholar calls "the most sublime, the most far-reaching, and the most majestic prayer found anywhere in Paul's Epistles, or possibly in the whole Bible." The prayer represents more than just one man interceding for a group of people. It represents God's deep longing for believers and the ultimate goal of redemption. Paul prays that the people might be "strengthened with might . . . in the inner man," that they might "comprehend" God's vastness and that they might "be filled with all the fullness of God." Quite an intercessory model for one-another praying.

HOW TO USE THIS BOOK

- The book is designed for a month with thirty-one days. You read and pray through a different "one another" passage each day of the month.
- You might read one *allelon* passage per week, stretching it for more than six months.
- You may want to read this book alone and pray for other believers as you read.
- You may choose to read this book with a group of believers, praying for one another.
- Each use of the word *allelon* is followed with four specific suggestions for prayer.
- Whichever approach you choose, our prayer for you is that this book will help you become more active and effective in fulfilling the biblical admonition to pray for one another.

Special recognition must be given to two who assisted with the preparation of this manuscript. Debbie Gillette has served as the Administrative Assistant to the Pastor at Wedgwood Baptist Church for seventeen years. Beverly Burrow is a former student, a friend, and an editorial specialist.

During three semesters, Southwestern Baptist Theological Seminary students read and critiqued these materials as a part of their studies in prayer.

In addition to this material being presented by Al Meredith at the Wedgwood Baptist Church in Fort Worth, Dan Crawford shared them in two Interim Pastorates—First Baptist Church in Decatur, Texas, and Central Baptist Church in Livingston, Texas. To members of these three churches who first heard these ideas, thanks is due.

Finally, to you who have begun to read this book, thanks for taking your prayer life to another level, a *one-another* level. Our prayer for you is that as you work your way through these pages, you will read and pray through whatever challenges may be present in or around your life. Blessings.

Now, before we get into the "one anothers" let's begin praying. Here are four suggestions to assist you in your intercessory prayers of today.

praying for one another

1. Spend some time today thanking God for the privilege of praying for others.

2. Make a list of five people for whom you can pray and commit to pray for them daily throughout this study of prayer.

3. Evaluate your past prayer life. What percentage has been intercession for others, and what percentage has been for yourself? How can you increase the intercession toward a more biblical percentage?

4. How many people do you know, for certain, are interceding for you? Do you need to recruit some intercessors who will pray faithfully for you?

Someone has well said, history belongs not to the power brokers, nor the politicians, nor the influence-wielders. History belongs to the intercessors.

It is the prayers of the saints that prompt God to act.

PRAY THAT WE WOULD PRAY FOR ONE ANOTHER
James 5:16

RECIPIENTS OF PRAYER

The shock in the aftermath of the September 15 shooting in our church was devastating as the media descended upon us and the world watched to see how we would respond. Our situation hit cyberspace via the Internet, and the result was that we became possibly the most prayed-for church in the world for a period of weeks. We received over 20,000 cards and letters and over 11,000 e-mails from around the world. Our Web site sustained more than 40,000 hits in the first few hours after the news broke. Literally, the world was on its knees for the believers at Wedgwood.

Because it was Wednesday of the national "See-You-At-The-Pole" event, there was a youth rally held at Wedgwood that evening. Youth from other churches were among the approximately one thousand people present in the church facilities that evening. Thus, prayer support was received from and shared with other churches involved by their presence.

Women in our church wallpapered the hallways of our church with these cards and letters and banners as the body of Christ lifted us up in prayer.

Words cannot express what encouragement we received from these heartfelt prayers for us in our hour of trial. We have spoken scores of times across the nation since then, telling the Wedgwood story, and everywhere we go, people ask us, "How are you folks doing? We have prayed so much for your church!"

The answer is, "We are doing well because you have been praying for us." Heaven alone will reveal the extent to which the prayers of the body of Christ have sustained us these past months and years.

Someone has well said, history belongs not to the power brokers, nor the politicians, nor the influence-wielders. History belongs to the intercessors.

INTERCESSION

In Revelation 8 we are given a glimpse of the scene in heaven as power and praise are ascribed to the Lamb upon the throne. All of a sudden the call is given for silence. The angels and seraphim cease their worship and praise as all of heaven comes to a halt. The cause—so the prayers of the saints can rise before Almighty God. Only then does the omnipotent God hand down judgment and fire on earth in response. It is the prayers of the saints that prompt God to act.

Jesus spent three years of His life here on earth teaching and preaching.

For the past 2,000 years, He has been involved in the primary task of interceding for His church. We would do well to intercede in a similar manner.

A recent survey showed that the average Christian spends four minutes per day in prayer and the average pastor spends seven minutes a day in prayer. Even then, some of the praying may be "amiss," according to James 4:3.

In a Peanuts cartoon, Charlie Brown is on his knees by his bed when Lucy enters. Charlie says, "I have a confession to make. I folded my hands upside down and got the opposite of what I prayed for." Improper prayer produces unacceptable results. Are you praying properly?

Why do we not actually "pray for one another" in a proper manner?

We do not know how to pray. Neither did the disciples, so they asked Jesus to teach them (Luke 11:1). The Lord's Prayer was the result.

We do not really believe that prayer accomplishes much. That's why, when we need something done, we first try to do it ourselves. Prayer becomes a last resort. Not so with Jesus in Luke 5:15-16.

We simply don't want to make the time for it. You make time for what is important. Prayer is just not a high priority. Contrast our priorities with Martin Luther's comment, "I have so much to do today, I need to spend two hours in prayer instead of one."

We are impatient. When we don't get an answer immediately, we stop praying. The "instant everything" generation has no time to "wait on God."

But James says, "pray for one another." Why? So "that you may be healed." And the reason is "the effective, fervent prayer of a righteous man avails much." James then illustrates his point with the story of Elijah—one who is like us (Jas. 5:17-18).

Pray that we would pray for one another.

Confess your trespasses to one another, and pray one for another, that you may be healed. The effective, fervent prayer of a righteous man avails much.

Jas. 5:16

praying for one another

1. Pray for your pastor and family—that God would deliver them from discouragement and shield them from attack.

2. Pray for the ministerial staff and lay leaders of your church—that God would unite their hearts and direct their efforts.

3. Pray for the Persecuted Church around the world—that God would give great grace for those who are suffering. Pray that they would persevere in such a way that many would be drawn to the Savior.

4. Pray that God would pour out the Holy Spirit upon the church in these last days and send a revival that would result in the glory of God and a harvest of souls.

Since we obviously would like to be spiritual salt in our world, we must pray for peace and harmony with one another.

The Society of International Law in London states that during the last 4,000 years there have been only 268 years of peace in spite of good peace treaties.

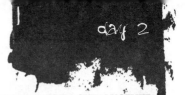

PRAY THAT WE WOULD BE AT PEACE WITH ONE ANOTHER
Mark 9:50

Greek mythology tells of Cadmus, who, while searching for his sister, met and killed a fierce dragon. He pulled the dragon's teeth and buried them in a field. But when he returned, he was dismayed to see that every tooth had grown into a fierce giant ominously blocking his way. What to do?

From behind a tree he threw a stone and hit one of the giants. The giant, thinking one of his brothers had done it, threw it back at him. A huge brawl ensued in which the giants killed or incapacitated each other. Thus, Cadmus was able to pass by safely on his way home.

When brothers fight, the Enemy is free to work.

SALT

The context of Mark 9:50 is about salt. Jesus concludes the teaching by saying that the disciples could not be the salt of the earth unless peace and harmony prevailed in their fellowship. Since we obviously would like to be spiritual salt in our world, we must pray for peace and harmony with one another.

The ancients proclaimed that there was nothing in the world purer than salt because it came from the two purest things, the sun and the sea. The very glistening of salt was a picture of purity. So we are to have within ourselves the purifying influence of Christ. As we are purified from selfishness, self-seeking, bitterness, anger, and grudge bearing and cleansed from irritation, moodiness, and self-centeredness, then and only then will we be able to live in peace with others. Only a life cleansed of self and filled with Christ can live in real fellowship with others.

Salt also preserves. Pray for one another that we would avoid contention, quarrels, struggles for places, honors, and offices and instead seek each other's welfare. Then we may think in terms of preserving our Christian witness in the world.

The Society of International Law in London states that during the last 4,000 years there have been only 268 years of peace in spite of good peace treaties. In the last three centuries, there have been 286 wars on the continent of Europe alone.

The Personnel Journal reported this incredible statistic: Since the beginning of recorded history, the entire world has been at peace less than eight percent of the time. In its study, the periodical discovered that of 3,530 years of recorded history, only 286 years saw peace. Moreover, in excess of

8,000 peace treaties were made—and broken.

A former president of the Norwegian Academy of Sciences and historians from England, Egypt, Germany, and India have come up with some startling information: since 3600 BC, the world has known only 292 years of peace! During this period there have been 14,351 wars, large and small, in which 3.64 billion people have been killed. The value of the property destroyed would pay for a golden belt around the world 97.2 miles wide and 33 feet thick. Since 650 BC there have also been 1,656 arms races, only sixteen of which have not ended in war. The remainder ended in the economic collapse of the countries involved.

PEACE

Long ago a man sought the perfect picture of peace. Not finding one that satisfied, he announced a contest to produce this masterpiece. The challenge stirred the imagination of artists everywhere, and paintings arrived from far and wide. Finally, the great day of revelation arrived. The judges uncovered one peaceful scene after another, while the viewers clapped and cheered. The tension grew. Only two pictures remained veiled. As a judge pulled the cover from one, a hush fell over the crowd. A mirror-smooth lake reflected lacy, green birches under the soft blush of the evening sky. Along the grassy shore, a flock of sheep grazed undisturbed. Surely this was the winner. The man with the vision uncovered the second painting himself, and the crowd gasped in surprise. Could this be peace? A tumultuous waterfall cascaded down a rocky precipice; the crowd could almost feel its cold, penetrating spray. Stormy-gray clouds threatened to explode with lightning, wind, and rain. In the midst of the thundering noises and bitter chill, a spindly tree clung to the rocks at the edge of the falls. One of its branches reached out in front of the torrential waters as if foolishly seeking to experience its full power. A little bird had built a nest in the elbow of that branch. Content and undisturbed in her stormy surroundings, she rested on her eggs. With her eyes closed and her wings ready to cover her little ones, she manifested peace that transcends all earthly turmoil.

Pray that believers will be at peace with one another, even in the midst of turmoil.

*Salt is good, but if the
salt loses its saltness,
how will you season it?
Have salt in yourselves, and
have peace one with another.*

Mark 9:50

praying for one another

1. Pray that God's Holy Spirit would call all believers together for the sake of reaching an unbelieving world (John 17:21).

2. Pray for peace within and between denominations and churches.

3. Pray that this present generation will conclude about God's church what the first century observed: "How they love one another!"

4. Pray that God will lead you to at least one friend from another church or denomination with whom you can develop a loving relationship.

True greatness lies not in outward honor, but in humble service.

We are not so much to gird ourselves with a towel as we are to strip ourselves of pride and position.

There is only one kind of greatness— the greatness of service.

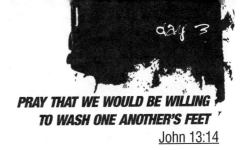

**PRAY THAT WE WOULD BE WILLING
TO WASH ONE ANOTHER'S FEET**
John 13:14

C.S. Lewis, the great Oxford scholar, has a chapter in his book *Mere Christianity* entitled "The Great Sin." In it he makes the case for pride as being the greatest sin of all. It was pride that kept the prodigal son in the pigsty of life so long. It was pride that brought sin, death, and hell into the human race as the enemy whispered, "You shall be as gods." It was pride that made Lucifer, the Star of the Morning, into the very devil himself ("I shall be like the Most High").

TRUE MINISTRY

Our generation is one of the most self-centered and self-seeking in history. Muhammad Ali shouted to the world, "I am the greatest!" The Beatles loudly claimed, "We're more popular than Jesus Christ." Fans at endless sports events raise their index fingers to the cameras and insist, "We're number one!"

Where is the heart of the Apostle Paul, who confesses, "I am the chief of sinners"?

Where is the heart attitude of John the Baptist, who prayed, "He must increase and I must decrease"?

Early in his ministry, D.L. Moody organized a Bible conference that brought in the best preachers from America and Europe. After the first night of inspiring worship and anointed preaching, he walked the corridors of the lodge and found that his European guests had set their boots outside their rooms to be polished overnight, as was the custom in Europe.

Not wanting to disappoint them, Moody went to several students and asked them to help. One replied, "Mr. Moody, I came here to study for the ministry, not to shine shoes." The others chimed in their agreement.

Moody could have exercised his rank as president and insisted, but he didn't. He graciously dismissed them to their rooms and then proceeded to polish the shoes himself.

TRUE GREATNESS

Jesus clearly told us, "The greatest of all is the servant of all." Then He demonstrated it by dying for all.

It was customary for the slave to wash the dusty, sandal-covered feet of the guests. On this day, the custom was set aside because the meal was likely held in a private home and thus no servant was present to wash the feet. According to Luke, a dispute had arisen earlier among the disciples over greatness (Luke 22:24). In response to the dispute, Jesus donned a towel to teach a lesson on real greatness. In the east, a towel around the waist was a sign and badge of slavery.

Jesus did for them what even a slave could not be forced to do. A host might do this as a voluntary act of hospitality, but no one could be forced to do it. Jesus lowered Himself to a place of servant and washed the feet of His disciples.

Having completed the act, Jesus drove home the lesson. If He had done this for them, they ought to do the same for one another. True greatness lies not in outward honor, but in humble service.

As long as they saw Him only as King, they would seek status for themselves as well. His purpose is to be an example. They were to keep doing as He had done for them. The example lay not in the form of the act, but in the spirit which prompted it. It is the principle of self-sacrificing service that is here enjoined, not the foot washing. To fulfill the command in a literal sense is a superficial interpretation that may even disregard the spirit behind the act.

Some observe foot washing as carefully as they do baptism and the Lord's Supper. Yet this practice is not an ordinance, but is cited as an example. We are not so much to gird ourselves with a towel as we are to strip ourselves of pride and position.

This passage must be interpreted in the context of culture. Some cultures no longer wash feet. Yet they still serve. The serious status seeker in the Kingdom of God eventually finds himself in the role of a servant. Like Teacher, like student.

Too often we stand on our own dignity when we ought to be kneeling at each other's feet. A player is pulled from the game and refuses to play anymore. A politician is overlooked for a prominent assignment and refuses to serve anymore. A church member wants his way—and he doesn't get it, so he puffs up and makes accusations and threats. A choir member is passed over for a big solo and refuses to sing again. Committees are selected, and someone omitted gets mad and broods. There is only one kind of greatness—the greatness of service.

Pray that we would be willing to serve one another in the spirit of Him who was willing to wash another's feet.

If I then, your Lord and Teacher,
have washed your feet,
you also ought to wash
one another's feet.

John 13:14

praying for one another

1. Pray that God will engender in you a humble, servant spirit.

2. Pray that humility will characterize church members, beginning with the pastor and other leaders, and that God will be glorified thereby.

3. Ask God to show you what acts of service you may perform for a brother or sister that would deeply bless them and could be kept secret from all but God.

4. Do the same for your family or close circle of friends.

What will channel life and health and happiness into the church? Sacrificial love.

While most of us will not be called to pay with our lives in some grand heroic moment, we are called to self-sacrificing acts of love.

PRAY THAT WE WOULD LOVE ONE ANOTHER
John 13:34-35; 15:12, 17; Romans 13:8;
Galatians 5:13; 1 Thessalonians 3:12;
4:9; 1 Peter 1:22; 1 John 3:11, 23;
4:7, 11-12; 2 John 5

LOVE, OLD AND NEW

Of the biblical references describing what we are to do for one another, eleven instruct us to love one another. Jesus' "new commandment" came as Judas left the Upper Room. Time was short. Now, the most crucial words must be spoken: "I will be with you only a little longer . . . (I give) a new commandment . . . love."

- 1 John 3:11—"For this is the message that we have heard from the beginning, that we should love one another."
- 1 John 3:23—"This is His commandment: that we should believe on the name of His son Jesus Christ and love one another, as He gave us commandment."
- 1 John 4:7—"Beloved, let us love one another, for love is of God and everyone who loves is born of God and knows God."
- 2 John 5—"Now I plead with you, lady, not as though I wrote a new commandment to you, but that which we have had from the beginning: that we love one another."

What caused
- Jesus to die on the cross? Love!
- Peter to preach with power on Pentecost after denial? Love!
- Paul to leave former associates and face death? Love!
- John to write so passionately even in exile? Love!
- Luther to defy the Roman church? Love!
- Livingston to face disease in Africa? Love!
- Judson to face poverty in India? Love!
- Lottie Moon to face starvation in China? Love!
- Bill Wallace to face death in China? Love!
- What will channel life and health and happiness into the church? Sacrificial love.

This is not really a new commandment. Leviticus 19:18 says the same thing—"you shall love your neighbor as yourself." The newness was the motivation—"as I have loved you."

How did Jesus love His disciples?

- Selflessly—Even our best attempts at love contain a part of self—what we get out of it. Not so with Jesus. His one desire was to give Himself to those whom He loved.
- Understandingly—Jesus knew the disciples. They had been together 24/7 for three years. He understood their moods, irritations, and weaknesses—yet still loved them.
- Forgivingly—Their leader was to deny Him. All would forsake Him. They never really understood Him. They were insensitive. Yet Jesus forgave them. Love that has not learned to forgive is very immature love. We tend to hurt those we love the most. Therefore, genuine love must include forgiveness.
- Realistically—You can't love everyone the same way. Anyone who attempts to do so will burn out quickly. Knowing this, Jesus set limits on His loving. One time He left a crying multitude on the shore and disappeared in a boat. But He had a special love for the twelve disciples. He gave them His best by being realistic about masses.
- Intimately—For three years, they did everything together—ate the same food, slept along the same roadsides, cried and laughed together, experienced good days (wedding feast) and bad days (clearing of the temple). There's not much intimacy in most churches today. We arrive in nice clothes, displaying learned smiles. We sit and listen and then go home—still hurting because no one really loved us.
- Intentionally—He chose to live with them. "Jesus went up on the mountain and called to Him those He Himself wanted. . . Then He appointed twelve that they might be with Him" (Mark 3:13-14). He made Himself available to them in a way in which He was not available to others.
- Sacrificially—There was no limit. No demand was too high or too much. If love meant the cross, so be it. He paid the ultimate price for love—"greater love has no man than this".

Charles Wesley wrote:

And can it be that I should gain an interest in the Savior's blood?
Died He for me, who caused His pain?
For me, who Him to death pursued?
Amazing love! How can it be that Thou, my God should die for me?

LOVE IN ACTION

On the Saturday after the Wednesday shooting tragedy at Wedgwood Baptist Church, we had the funerals of four of our dearest people. The streets around our church had become a parking lot for satellite trucks as the world watched to see how God's church would handle grief of this magnitude. We were determined to worship together on Sunday. The carpet had been torn up and bullet holes and gouges from the bomb left our worship center in shambles. How would we make things presentable when we were at non-stop funerals?

Saturday morning, during the funerals that were being held elsewhere, a group from a neighboring Church of Christ arrived and asked, "Is there anything we can do?" Our administrator asked if they would be so kind as to help him clean up. For hours these people swept and mopped and scrubbed and straightened our sanctuary in readiness for the Lord's Day. Nothing was in it for them except the satisfaction of knowing they had obeyed God and loved His people.

On that Sunday morning, our normal Prayer Watch group of a dozen or so had swollen to over two hundred prayer warriors from across the city. A church in Tulsa, Oklahoma—five hours away—sent a van full of people to prayer-walk the property while we were in worship before the Lord and before a watching world.

While most of us will not be called to pay with our lives in some grand heroic moment, we are called to self-sacrificing acts of love. It might mean giving up your special pew for a newcomer who didn't know that that was your seat; or parking farther from the door so others might have better access; or laying down your personal taste in worship styles so that others might be drawn to God by a style with which they are more familiar.

Pray that we would love one another.

praying for one another

1. Rejoice in the fact that, no matter what, as a child of God nothing you can say or do will ever cause God to love you any more or less than He does right now.

2. Ask God to reveal to you several of the less lovable in your fellowship and lead you to show a simple, self-sacrificing act of love on their behalf.

3. Ask God to lead you to someone of another church or denomination and, by some distinctive act of mercy, demonstrate God's love for them.

4. Ask God to give you the grace never to publicly unjustly criticize another child of God, in order that the world might know that Jesus is the Christ (John 17:21).

*No member of the body
can function alone.*

PRAY THAT WE WOULD BE MEMBERS OF ONE ANOTHER
Romans 12:5

In an American city, there is a church building displaying the sign "The Perfect Church." To join it would be to ruin its name. There is no perfect church because all churches are composed of imperfect people like us. BUT, imperfect as we are—"we are members of one another."

MEMBERS BY FAITH

The only way we are members of one another is that we are members in Him. We are not members by race, nor by color, nor by location, nor by denomination, nor by income, but by personal faith.

We are "members" of "one body." The "body" is not a local congregation. It is not a denomination. It is believers—those like us and those unlike us. There may be more sitting at the table than we have been sharing bread with.

The word "members" implies unity and diversity—characteristics also seen in the physical body. Diversity without unity is disorder, while unity without diversity is monotonous.

The body must be cooperative. The right hand must never fight the left hand. There are no majority parts. The third verse of "Onward Christian Soldiers" says, "We are not divided, all one body we."

We live in a relational world. Relating implies a reciprocal experience. We are interdependent members of one another. Each must be able to say, "I am receiving from other members." Some think this is a sign of spiritual weakness and prefer to handle the job personally. Yet God chooses to meet many of our needs through others.

Paul, the most spiritually mature person in the New Testament, desired a relationship with others. On one occasion he wrote, "When we could no longer endure it, we thought it good to be left in Athens alone" (1 Thess. 3:1). For Paul, being alone was a last resort.

MEMBERS WITH SPECIFIC GIFTS

Each must also be able to say, "I am contributing to other members." To this end God has gifted each believer (Rom. 12:6-8; 1 Cor. 12; Eph. 4; 1 Pet. 4) for the purpose of "building up of the body of Christ" (Eph. 4:12, NASB). No member of the body can function alone. No body member is more important than another (Rom. 12:3). There is one body with many members, and no one person is the entire body.

Work hard at creating and maintaining unity in the body:

- The "body is a unit made up of many parts" (1 Cor. 12:12).
- "Agree with one another so there is no division in the body" (1 Cor. 1:10).
- "Make every effort to keep the unity of Spirit" (Eph. 4:3).

The relationship also carries a warning concerning expectations. Don't be a perfectionist with yourself. There is always room for improvement. A plaque on an office wall proclaims, "Above a healthy discipline, be gentle on yourself."

Don't be a perfectionist with others. We often have merciless standards by which we evaluate others. When you insist on all or nothing with other fallen people, you usually get more nothing, rather than all.

Different members of the body perform different functions. Some, like the eyes, perhaps are more obvious and therefore more appreciated. We write songs about the eyes of the ones we love—loving eyes, adoring eyes, mysterious eyes.

Other members of the body are less obvious—the kidneys, for instance. No one writes songs about kidneys! But have you ever had a kidney stone? That will get your attention! Have you ever visited a dialysis center? People there fully understand and appreciate healthy, functioning kidneys.

The point is that every member or part of our body has a specific function it has been designed to carry out. There are no unnecessary parts. All are needed.

So why do eighty percent of church members have no ministry beyond occupying a specific pew one day a week? Why do ninety percent of church members not know what their spiritual gifts are?

In the days following the shooting at Wedgwood Baptist Church, men mowed the pastor's lawn without being asked. Women washed clothes for the pastor's family and kept the house straightened, especially helpful when the Governor and the Mayor "dropped by." A seminary student drove the pastor to and from the funerals and interviews. A former youth pastor flew in from Nashville to help with the counseling and encourage the current youth pastor. People with the gift of mercy camped out at hospitals. Others spackled and painted the walls of our sanctuary. And many prayed.

Pray that we would be members of one another.

. . . so we, being many,
are one body in Christ,
and every one members
of one another.

Rom. 12:5

praying for one another

1. Pray that God would reveal to you and to others in your church what your spiritual gifts are.

2. Pray that, on the basis of your giftedness, God will lead you to the ministry prepared for you.

3. Pray that your church would be revitalized as people seek to serve one another.

4. Pray that your pastor would be an effective (or more effective) "Equipper" of the body, and that people will respond to pastoral leadership.

*Spiritually, we are brothers
with those who, like us,
have been born again.*

*Devotion and honor take time,
but the maturity is worth it.*

PRAY THAT WE WOULD BE DEVOTED TO ONE ANOTHER
Romans 12:10 (NIV)

A man's wife was terminally ill, on hospice care. The husband asked the hospice worker how he could show proper devotion and honor for his wife. Then he had an idea.

He called the family together. He dressed his wife in her wedding dress, put on a tuxedo and tie, brought flowers into the room, and arranged for a videotape of the ceremony. With the family gathered around the bedside, the husband announced "I just wanted everyone to know, I still do."

DEVOTION COMMANDED

When we are helpless and hurting, Jesus still offers us His devotion and honor. We should also be devoted to one another, honoring one another. Both ideas are found in Romans 12:10.

In the King James Version of the Bible, "devoted" is translated as "kindly affectioned." It is the only time this Greek word is used in the New Testament. The word refers to "love within family." We are to be devoted like a family. It blends together the idea of family with the idea of brotherly love.

- 1 Thessalonians 4:9—"Concerning brotherly love . . . love one another."
- Hebrews 13:1—"Let brotherly love continue."
- 1 Peter 1:22—"Since you have purified your souls in obeying the truth through the Spirit in sincere love of the brethren, love one another fervently with a pure heart."
- 1 Peter 3:8—"Finally all of you be of one mind, having compassion for one another; love as brothers."
- 2 Peter 1:7—"Add to your faith virtue, to virtue knowledge, to knowledge self-control, to self-control perseverance, to perseverance godliness, to godliness brotherly kindness and to brotherly kindness love."

"Kindly" comes from same root word as "kindred" and further emphasizes family love. Many love the brethren, but too few are kindly affectioned toward them.

"With brotherly love." Again, the Greek word means the love of brothers. It is used 230 times in the New Testament to refer to the Christian family. It literally means "from the same womb." Spiritually, we are brothers with those who, like us, have been born again. This brotherly love fulfills Christ's new commandment "love one another." It struggles in immaturity like young children do, but grows strong in maturity.

DEVOTION UNDESERVED

The philosopher Arthur Schopenhauer once said, "I could take Jesus Christ a lot easier if He did not insist I receive His leprous bride, the Church, as well."

But that's the deal. Jesus says, "Love Me, love My bride."

How should I respond if someone comes to me and pours praises upon me for my preaching, my care for the flock and my administrative skills, but then starts in on criticizing my wife, as a sorry no account excuse for a woman? I can tell you this—they'd better be ready to duck! Love me, love my wife.

God's love for His church is not based on her irresistible charm and beauty. It was "while we were yet sinners" that He loved and died for us. If you are waiting for the church to be deserving of your devotion, it will never happen. I am devoted to my children not because they are always perfectly lovable, but because they are mine! Sometimes we disappoint one another, but our devotion to one another doesn't cease because of our disappointment. The measure of our devotion is the size of the disappointment it takes to cause us to abandon one another.

There are at least two things in the world you cannot do alone. One is be married. There must be someone else who, when you say, "I do," responds with "Me, too."

And you cannot be a Christian alone. We need each other. No matter how important and disappointing we may be at times to one another, nothing must hinder our devotion to each other.

A man accompanied a friend home one evening and was amazed at how he treated his wife with such devotion. "How was your day?" "Dinner smells good." "You look great." So he decided to go home and try it with his wife. No sooner had he begun than his wife began to cry. "Our son got in a fight at school, the refrigerator quit, the car won't start, and now you come home drunk." Devotion, when lacking over a long period of time, may be difficult to recognize when it resurfaces, but resurface it must.

Devotion and honor take time, but the maturity is worth it.

Pray that we would be devoted to one another.

Be devoted to one another
in brotherly love. . . .

Rom. 12:10 (NIV)

praying for one another

1. Pray that God will draw out the poison of the bitter disappointment that other saints may have given you through the years.

2. Pray that God will lead you to perform a loving act of devotion this week to one of the often-overlooked members of your local body of believers.

3. Pray that your congregation will cultivate a reputation like that of the early church, of whom it was said, "Oh, how they love one another!"

4. Identify someone in your fellowship who is "devoted" to you. If you can name no such person, what would you need to do to cause someone to be "devoted" to you?

Many church problems arise and fester because someone was not given the proper honor.

One of the real problems in the church is that everyone wants to play quarterback.

The Bible is clear. Saints should be concerned that others receive honor.

PRAY THAT WE WOULD HONOR ONE ANOTHER
Romans 12:10 (NIV)

To "honor" or "give preference to one another" carries two meanings. It means both to take the lead in showing honor and to give the other person the higher place. Both meanings are good. Either is correct. No one is absolutely sure which is meant in Romans 12:10. Biblical examples of this concept abound.

- Luke 14:10—"When you are invited, go and sit down in the lowest place, so that when he who invited you comes he may say, 'Friend, go up higher.' Then you will have glory in the presence of those who sit at the table with you."
- Philippians 2:3—"Let nothing be done through selfish ambition or conceit, but in lowliness of mind let each esteem others better than himself."

TABLE TALK

Many church problems arise and fester because someone was not given the proper honor. They were neglected or unappreciated. Ego took over, and they reacted.

Shortly before His death, Jesus was teaching His disciples a powerful lesson related to honor. In the Upper Room, as the heart of Jesus was aching with what He knew was coming, the disciples jockeyed with one another for the best seat around the table. No one noticed an unconscionable and unbearable omission. No one was willing to perform what was a task for a slave. Then, to their astonishment, Jesus strips down to His loin-cloth, dons a towel, kneels before them, and begins to wipe the filth of the day from their feet (John 13:12-16).

John addressed the letter of 3 John to Gaius, a beloved friend, rather than addressing it to Diotrephes, who loved to be put first and have pre-eminence. A *Who's Who in the Bible* says of Diotrephes: "a peevishly ambitious person brought into prominence entirely by his obstinate refusal to recognize properly constituted authority in the church." A better example of honor is Gaius, the model of devotion.

EGOS VS. HONOR

Not too many people have ever heard of Jeff van Note. For sixteen years, he was the starting center for the astoundingly mediocre Atlanta

Falcons football team. No one ever gave him credit for winning the game. He never dominated the headlines.

The offensive center, you see, has two primary tasks: (1) to snap the ball effectively and (2) to take on middle linebackers, the monsters of the game. For sixteen years he had to deal with the likes of Dick Butkus and Jack Lambert, who enjoyed destroying plays and the people who try to carry them out.

The only time the center's name is ever mentioned is when he messes up with a bad snap or gets called for a holding penalty. Van Note was quoted once as saying, "the biggest compliment you can give me is to elect my quarterback to the All-Pro team."

That is the essence of what it means to "in honor give preference to one another."

One of the real problems in the church is that everyone wants to play quarterback. There once was a man who hadn't been to church in twenty years because his name had been overlooked in the recognition service for the building program. Nietzsche observed, "If it weren't for bronze plaques, half the cathedrals in Europe would be unfinished."

The Bible is clear. Saints should be concerned that *others* receive honor.

The church in Rome had problems with a spirit of competition. So the Apostle Paul begins this practical section of the epistle with the command "not to think more highly of himself than he ought to think."

It seems as though half of us suffer from terribly low self-images. In a show of pseudo-spirituality, we lament, "I am nothing," and that is what we accomplish for the kingdom. The other half suffers from a distressingly high self-image or over-inflated ego that demands attention, appreciation, and recognition. To a narcissistic church, God says, "seek out one another and bestow praise."

May God bless His church with more people like Giovanni di Bernardone, son of Don Pietro, who was rescued from a life of self-indulgence by painful wounds suffered and borne in a hospital. There he learned, "It's not about me."

Francisco, as he was called, received a vision of rebuilding broken down churches and ministering to the poor, the sick, the hungry, and the lepers. And so he did. When his merchant father returned from a business trip, he found Francisco *giving* away all his merchandise. He totally disowned his son on the spot.

Francisco walked away to a life of serving and honoring others, and the Medieval Church was revived. History knows him as Saint Francis of Assisi.

Pray that we would honor one another.

*Honor one another
above yourselves.*

Rom. 12:10 NIV

praying for one another

1. Pray that God will show you opportunities to honor someone else, then do it.

2. Pray that God will reveal and heal old wounds where you were overlooked.

3. Find a way to express praise and recognition for the most significant people in your life: spouse, parents, children, and others.

4. Pray for the "irregular" people in your life, those who tend to "rub you the wrong way," that God would pour out His blessings upon them and they might be deeply honored.

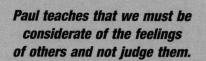

Paul teaches that we must be considerate of the feelings of others and not judge them.

The plethora of Protestant denominations is due in many respects to our inability to refrain from judging our brothers.

PRAY THAT WE WOULD NOT JUDGE ONE ANOTHER
Romans 14:13

In the cartoon sitcom, *The Simpsons*, the family's conservative Christian neighbor, Ed Flanders, tells Homer, "We've been away to a Christian camp. We've been learning how to become more judgmental."

OUR JUDGMENTAL LABEL

Why is it that American Evangelicals have come to be known not for the grace, love, and forgiveness we say God has granted to us, but rather for harsh, judgmental, unforgiving attitudes? Like twenty-first-century Santas, we're "making a list and checking it twice."

- Real Christians don't wear make up—this repeated most often by those who need it most.
- Real Christians won't smoke a cigarette after dinner—but a half-gallon of ice cream before bedtime is allowable.
- Real Christians never consider divorce—murder, perhaps, but never divorce.

The problem with reducing our faith to a list of rules is that it results in one of two devastating consequences—either *shame* if you break the rules, or *pride* when you don't. There is no need for shame for anyone who is in Christ, for the good news is "There is therefore now no condemnation to those who are in Christ Jesus" (Rom. 8:1). And of all the sins God sets Himself against, none is so prevalent nor so odious to God as pride. "God resists the proud" (Jas. 4:6).

Jesus reserved His worst epithets for the religious leaders of His day who condemned others for not living up to their list of rules. He called these toxic leaders "hypocrites . . . blind guides . . . fools . . . serpents . . . vipers" (Matt. 23:15-33).

TWO ROMAN ISSUES

This same type of spiritual abuse was being practiced in the early church at Rome. The issue there was whether or not to eat meat or to observe certain days. Those who ate meat freely belittled and condemned those whose conscience would not allow them to. Those who refused it felt others were licentious. Those who observed certain days were critical of those who did not.

Paul clearly addresses both groups as equally guilty when he writes, "Let us stop judging one another." The word "judge" is in the present active subjunctive tense in Greek, meaning we must not continue in the habit of judging one another. Here Paul echoes the teaching of Jesus in the Sermon on the Mount, "Judge not, that you be not judged" (Matt. 7:1). Instead of judging, Paul encourages resolution of the issues that tend to create a "stumbling block," causing others to fall.

The Stoics believed there were things that were, of themselves, indifferent—neither good nor bad. They said it all depends on the handle by which you pick them up. A piece of art to one person might be a genuine work of art, while to another it might be obscene. To one person a discussion might be stimulating, while to another it might be boring. A particular type of activity might be enjoyable to one and dull to another. In each case it is not the art or discussion or activity that is good or bad, but the perspective of the individual.

Here Paul is responding to two issues: eating meat and observing certain days. He says, it is not the meat nor the day that is the issue, for meat and days are indifferent. It is the perspective of the individual. To the strong believer, eating meat or observing certain days might not be bad, but to a new believer, these could be unacceptable.

While we must not allow others to dictate our choices, Paul teaches that we must be considerate of the feelings of others and not judge them. Neither should we continue in some activity that creates a stumbling block for others.

A MATTER OF ACCEPTANCE

In the body of Christ, we are to accept one another unconditionally. Every generation throughout church history has had to deal with this issue. In the fourth century, they argued whether those who had recanted under persecution could be allowed back into the church. The disagreement even turned violent.

During the Reformation, after virulent "pamphlet wars" the discussion spilled over onto the battlefield in the Religious Wars of the sixteenth century.

More recently Orthodox and Catholic priests have come to blows in Jerusalem over who gets to refurbish the Church of the Resurrection. And the plethora of Protestant denominations is due in many respects to our inability to refrain from judging our brothers.

A rather recent country song had the man excusing his shortcomings and begging for non-judgmental mercy by saying he was "a work in progress." Surely we can treat other believers with equal non-judgmental mercy and allow them to be works in progress.

Pray that we would "not judge one another."

*Therefore let us not judge
one another anymore,
but rather resolve this,
that no one put a stumbling block or
a cause to fall in his brother's way.*

Rom. 14:13

praying for one another

1. Ask God to reveal to your heart people you have "written off" because of something they may have said or done.

2. Ask God to allow you to see them as He does—fellow saints for whom He died.

3. Take the time to express your gratitude for God's patience and grace in your life.

4. Remember that we are all "Works in progress."

> *The God who created every snowflake to be unique does not demand that all children look and act the same. God loves variety!*

> *Any plan for world evangelism that does not take into consideration interdenominational cooperation is doomed to fail.*

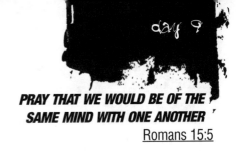

PRAY THAT WE WOULD BE OF THE SAME MIND WITH ONE ANOTHER
Romans 15:5

"Sometimes you want to go where everybody knows your name. . . ."

Can you hear the theme song from the once-popular television show *Cheers*? Unfortunately, it is about a bar, not a church. The truth is that everyone wants to be agreed with and accepted.

A casual study of church history reveals one of Satan's best methods for destroying the church—namely, destroying the unity among believers. He is skilled at creating confusion, insensitivity, and division. The best weapon against this is "like-mindedness."

AN ATTITUDE OF UNITY

"Like-mindedness" is an interesting biblical concept. The Greek word means "to think the same thing; united." It does not mean that everybody ought to be of the same opinion about everything, all of the time. Someone has well said, "If we both agree on everything, one of us is unnecessary."

The word here for "mind" is not the usual Greek word *"nous,"* but the word *"phane."* The term originally referred to one's midsection. Perhaps the Greeks once thought that thinking was done with the stomach. Eventually, however, the phrase came to mean one's intellect, especially one's *attitude*.

Have you ever noticed how critical one's attitude is? Do you remember this nursery rhyme?

"Pussy cat, pussy cat, where have you been?
I've been to London to visit the Queen!
Pussy cat, pussy cat, what saw you there?
I saw a little mouse under her chair?"

The Tower of London, Big Ben, the Crown Jewels, and all that cat noticed was a rodent under the throne? Our attitude determines our outlook.

A SPIRIT OF UNITY

When God calls us to like-mindedness, the call is not for complete and perfect unanimity. Nor does God require total uniformity. The God who created every snowflake to be unique does not demand that all children look and act the same. God loves variety! Nor does like-mindedness mean ecclesiastical union. Mark Twain once put two cats into a bag and hung it from a clothesline. There was union in that bag, but don't mistake the screeching for unity.

No, like-mindedness is a unity in spirit and essential purpose. We can differ on music styles, times of worship, evangelistic methods, economic status, political values, and even some doctrines. But our ultimate purpose is "to glorify and enjoy God forever."

In the high priestly prayer of Jesus, He prayed for unity. "Holy Father, keep through Your name those whom You have given Me, that they may be one as we are one." Then Jesus prayed for the unity of all future believers. "I do not pray for these alone but also for those who will believe in Me . . . that they may all be one" (John 17:11-23).

Paul shared this plea for like-mindedness with others as well:

- To Rome—"Be of the same mind toward one another" (Rom. 5:16).
- To Corinth—"I plead with you . . . that there be no divisions among you, but that you be perfectly joined together in the same mind and in the same judgment" (1 Cor. 1:10).
- To Ephesus—"Make every effort to keep the unity of the Spirit through the bond of peace" (Eph. 4:3).
- To Philippi—"stand firm in one spirit, contending as one man for the faith of the Gospel" (Phil. 1:27).
- To Philippi—"fulfill my joy by being like-minded, having the same love, being of one accord, of one mind" (Phil. 2:2).

This concept is likewise demonstrated in the church at Jerusalem:

- "Day by day, continuing with one mind" (Acts 2:46).
- Because of their "unity" they enjoyed "the favor of all the people" and "the Lord added to their number" (Acts 2:47).
- Widows were being neglected in the distribution of food, but when unity was restored, "the Word of God spread and the number of disciples increased rapidly" (Acts 6:7).

The world will never believe, to any great extent, that Jesus is the Christ so long as His followers are divided in spirit and publicly wrangling with one another. Any plan for world evangelism that does not take into consideration interdenominational cooperation is doomed to fail. No question is more difficult to answer, nor asked more frequently in witnessing than the non-Christian asking about the disunity among Christians. When we foster disunity, we are shooting the body in the foot.

Pray that we would be of the same mind with one another.

*Now may the God of patience
and consolation grant you
to be like-minded toward one another,
according to Christ Jesus. . . .*

Rom. 15:5

praying for one another

1. Pray that God will reveal to you and the members of your church the true non-negotiables of the faith that we have in common with one another.

2. Pray that God will unite the hearts of the people in your church with a common love for Christ and desire to see Him glorified, and that other differences might be laid aside for that purpose.

3. Think of the people in your church who are most different in looks, tastes, customs, and preferences and thank God that He has brought them into fellowship with you.

4. Pray for other churches and denominations that God would bless and prosper them and be glorified thereby. Pray for their pastors by name.

Accepting one another doesn't stop once we've shaken hands during the "Welcome Time" in Sunday morning worship.

PRAY THAT WE WOULD RECEIVE ONE ANOTHER
Romans 15:7

The word "receive" means to "enthusiastically welcome." It is the same word used in Acts 28:2 when the residents of Malta "received" Paul after his shipwreck. It is the same word used in Philemon 1:17 to describe how believers should "receive" the runaway slave Onesimus. In some translations, the word "receive" is rendered "accept."

In the Greek present tense, "receive" implies continuous action. Also in the imperative mood, "receive" is an order from our Commander-in-Chief. There are no options, no Plan B. "Keep on enthusiastically receiving one another." Accepting one another doesn't stop once we've shaken hands during the "Welcome Time" in Sunday morning worship.

THE EARLY CHURCH

There were two problems in the church at Rome that prompted this command. One was the problem of legalism as addressed in Romans 14. There are many gray areas in life that the Scriptures do not directly address—skirt length, hairstyle, watching movies.

In the early church, the issue was whether or not to eat meat that had been offered to idols. To some it was a matter of good stewardship—it was good meat at cheap prices. To others it involved what they thought was sinful accommodation. Those strong in the faith felt they were free in Christ to partake. Newer Christians were fearful they might be contaminated. Their consciences were violated. Paul's answer to both parties was to follow their own convictions, but to "accept [or receive] one another."

The second problem in the early church was that of partiality or prejudice. In Romans 12:16, Paul says, "Do not set your mind on high things, but associate with the humble." The early church was guilty of prejudices: economic (Jas. 2), racial (Gal. 2), religious (Acts 15). The Bible is clear: "if you show partiality, you commit sin" (Jas. 2:9).

Rejection often arises from a prideful heart. Where is your pride? In your pedigree? Jesus was considered the illegitimate child of a poor carpenter. In your good looks? It was said of Jesus that "he has no form or comeliness . . . no beauty that we should desire Him" (Isa. 53:2). In your reputation? Jesus was known as a glutton, a winebibber, and a friend of sinners. In your degrees? Jesus had no formal academic training. In your popularity? Jesus "came to His own, and His own did not receive Him" (John 1:11).

Many of us grew up in an era when you were accepted by other Christians based on how well you functioned with the "Do and Don't Do" list.

- ■ Do be at church at least four times per week.
- ■ Do bring your Bible to church.
- ■ Do keep quiet in worship services.
- ■ Don't date anyone but Christians.
- ■ Don't smoke, drink, dance, or chew.

While the Bible does give us "dos" and "don'ts" they are often far different from cultural "dos" and "don'ts." If God accepts me, why would fellow believers not accept me? We strive to glorify God. We "do" whatever it takes to glorify God and "don't" do those things that keep glory from God.

THE CHURCH TODAY

The same two things that affected the early church—legalism and prejudice—trouble us today. In that day, it was eating meat that had been offered to idols. In our day, it is a laundry list of actions.

Many things make us different from one another. Too often we focus on these. We have more in common that can enable us, when willing, to accept one another. The ultimate purpose is "to glorify God," that is, "to bring praise to God."

It wasn't as if the boy were mean or slow or ugly. It was just that he didn't *fit*. He tried to fit in, to find his place of acceptance in the youth group. The pastor tried to take him and other boys under his wing. He called them his "preacher boys" and took them with him to rallies and conferences and let them take turns reading Scripture, leading music, and even preaching. But somehow Larry just didn't fit in, didn't feel part of the group.

He never married. He enlisted in the military but was mustered out without commendation. He grew more isolated and, subsequently, increasingly paranoid.

Eventually, shortly after his father's death, he just could not take it anymore. His lonely, paranoid heart led him to take two guns and a pipe bomb into a youth rally at Wedgwood Baptist Church and open fire. When he was finished, seven were seriously wounded, seven others were dead . . . and then Larry Gene Ashbrook took his own life.

How crucial it is that we learn to accept one another.

Pray that we would accept one another.

Therefore receive one another,
just as Christ also received us,
to the glory of God.

Rom. 15:7

praying for one another

1. Pray that God will reveal to you the people on the periphery of activities in your church who need someone to reach out in an act of acceptance.

2. Thank God, who knows every shameful deed and every evil thought in your heart, yet still receives you as "accepted in the Beloved" (Eph. 1:6).

3. Pray that God would engender a spirit of openness, transparency, and acceptance in your church.

4. Pray that God would forgive all the times and ways we have excluded others from fellowship in the body of Christ.

Admonishment in the body of Christ must be both confrontive and caring, depending on the nature of the problem.

PRAY THAT WE WOULD ADMONISH ONE ANOTHER
Romans 15:14

The various translations of this verse are confusing. The King James Version, the New King James Version, and the New American Standard Bible all translate the Greek word as "admonish." Williams translation uses "counsel one another." The Beck translation translates it "correct one another." The New International Version reads "instruct one another."

MEANING OF ADMONISHMENT

The Greek word does not refer to a casual communication, nor even to normal teaching. It implies a definite exhortation, correction, and warning.

When the same Greek word is used in 1 Thessalonians 5:14, Acts 20:31, and 1 Corinthians 4:14, it is a more definite warning—not toward the goal of punishment, but of correction.

The warning here is to "stop passing judgment on one another" (Rom. 14:13). But how can they carry out this warning and not judge one another? That's why "instruction" is needed.

The early Christians were competent to "instruct one another" because they were "complete in knowledge." Instruction must be based on God's will and way, not on what we think. If we are not knowledgeable of God's Word, we ourselves are in need of instruction. "Knowledge" will often keep one from judging.

METHOD OF ADMONISHMENT

Here are some practical "instructions":

- *Do it in love.* "For three years I never stopped warning each of you night and day with tears" (Acts 20:31).
- *Make it personal.* Some pastors preach to the entire congregation (or teachers to an entire class) hoping to "hit" one person who is in need of a specific instruction. When the Bible speaks of "public rebuke," it does so only after personal confrontation (Matt. 18:15-17; 1 Tim. 5:19).
- *Make it persistent.* Again, Paul instructed "night and day" for "three years" (Acts 20:31).
- *Be sure your motives are pure.* In 1 Corinthians 4:14, Paul states his motive: "I am not writing this to shame you, but to warn you, as my dear children."
- *Be sure the goal is proper.* There is only one proper goal—to help indi-

viduals become mature in Christ. Paul wrote, "We proclaim Him, instructing/warning/admonishing everyone with all wisdom, so that we may present everyone perfect in Christ" (Col. 1:28-29).

- *Balance the instruction/warning.* Here Paul speaks of corrective instruction/warning. In Colossians 3:16, Paul writes of preventive admonishment, instruction, warning. Both are needed.
- *Evaluate your own life before instructing/warning others.* Is it "full of goodness" and "complete in knowledge"? Galatians 6:1 warns us to consider "yourself lest you also be tempted." Our attitude must not be haughty or holier than thou.

MODEL OF ADMONISHMENT

Paul often instructed them with his own model. He told them they were "competent to instruct one another," first because they were "full of goodness." They were competent to instruct one another because they were living holy lives of Christlikeness. They were mature enough to make sure they removed the "logs" from their own eyes before they tried to remove the "speck" from another's eye. "Full of goodness" will keep one from judging.

Admonishment in the body of Christ must be both confrontive and caring, depending on the nature of the problem. The downhearted and brokenhearted need a word of encouragement and comfort (2 Cor. 1:4). The rebellious and cold-hearted need to be challenged and corrected (Gal. 6:1); the confused need to be instructed.

Never has there been a generation with more television and radio programs on counseling, more books on mental and emotional health, more seminars and professional counselors. And yet, never has there been a generation more confused, broken, lonely, depressed, and generally unhappy.

While there is a place for specialized counselors and therapists, many of our emotional and spiritual needs could be met if the members of the body of Christ would simply care enough to confront one another. One of the greatest plagues of the modern church is the mind-your-own-business attitude that refuses to get involved in one another's lives, refuses to get involved in loving accountability with one another.

One of the characteristics that marked Wedgwood Baptist Church in the weeks following the shooting was the fact that no one seemed to want to go home following the services. People would stay and talk for hours. While other churches were canceling Sunday evening worship services, Wedgwood went to a ninety-minute service with a full house. People wanted to get involved with one another—encouraging, comforting, challenging instructing, possibly even correcting one another.

The secret of the explosive growth of early Methodism was the forming of spiritual cell groups who methodically (thus, the name) held each other accountable in their personal lives. From the pastor in the pulpit to the person in the pew, we all need folks who love us enough to admonish and encourage us.

Pray that we would admonish one another.

And I myself am, also confident concerning you, my brethren, that you also are full of goodness, filled with all knowledge, able also to admonish one another.

Rom. 15:14

praying for one another

1. Pray that God will give you a circle of Christian friends with whom you can be transparent and who will lovingly hold you accountable.

2. Pray that God will provide accountability partners for your pastor and staff.

3. Pray that God will reveal to your heart any "secret sins" that have crept into your life unaware, and then send loving friends to confirm that conviction.

4. Pray that God will lead you in helping other friends and loved ones become aware of areas in their lives that God wants to change. Pray for courage and compassion as the Spirit leads you to lovingly admonish them.

Principles are biblical and timeless.
Methods are cultural and temporal.

day 12

PRAY THAT WE WOULD GREET ONE ANOTHER
Romans 16:16;
1 Corinthians 16:20;
1 Peter 5:14

The article told of Kimberly Livingston, age thirty-nine who had died two months earlier. For fifty-nine days, officials waited for someone to claim her body before burying her in an unmarked grave.

Overheard in an area funeral home as a couple came out of a viewing room, "I can't believe no one else came."

How tragic to be unclaimed and unwanted in death. How much more tragic to be unnoticed and uncared for in life.

EARLY CHURCH EXAMPLES

Three different New Testament churches received instruction related to this type of one anothering. Paul sent a greeting to Priscilla and Aquila and to the church that met in their house (Rom. 16:3-5), and then for the next few verses listed twenty-six names and descriptions of mostly unknown people. These names represent a diverse church, transcending race, culture, and gender. The list includes

- The first Asian convert
- Many women
- A countryman of Paul
- One with a Roman name
- One with an imperial household name
- One from Jewish nobility
- One whose name meant "Persian woman"
- Some with common slave names

All were to be greeted. None were to be ignored because of their differences. (For the other two examples, see 1 Corinthians 16:20 and 1 Peter 5:14.)

A HOLY KISS

The admonition to "greet one another" was a part of their worship. Justin Martyr, describing Christians of the second century wrote, "When we have ceased from our prayers, we mutually salute one another by a kiss, and then we bring forward the bread and the cup." Their method was "a holy kiss," or as other translations say, "Salute one another."

The Phillips translation offers a British slant, "Have a hearty handshake all around." Some of us used to sing, "Shake another hand, shake the hand next to you."

This is a good example of principle and method. The principle is to "greet one another." The method is "with a holy kiss." Principles are biblical and timeless. Methods are cultural and temporal.

There are other examples of this principle/method idea. In Acts 2, Peter was preaching in a loud voice. He had to do so because there was no amplification system. The principle was to proclaim the gospel. The method was with a loud voice.

A "holy kiss" is different from a passionate kiss or even an affectionate kiss. All participated, even men with men and women with women. This command is repeated at least five times in the New Testament. We would do well to take it seriously. Biblical examples of a "holy kiss" may be found in:

- Luke 15:20—Father and prodigal son
- Acts 20:37—"They wept aloud and embraced Paul and kissed him"
- 1 Corinthians 16:20; 2 Corinthians 13:12—"Greet one another with a holy kiss"
- 1 Thessalonians 5:16—"Greet all the brethren with a holy kiss"
- 1 Peter 5:14—"a holy kiss of love"

So often our modern methods of greeting one another are cavalier and insincere. We ask, "How ya doin'?" but we don't really want to hear the answer. We have enough problems of our own. Even our custom of shaking hands arose from fear and guardedness. In medieval times one's right hand was his sword hand, so to reach out and grip each other's right hand was to ensure relative safety, for the moment, at least.

The point is to be sure to greet and welcome one another warmly and sincerely.

LEON TROTSKY

After the Russian Revolution of 1905 was crushed by the Tsarist regime, one of the leaders, Leon Trotsky, fled the country for his life and eventually wound up in America. He was confused, searching for meaningful answers, in need of direction.

In this state of mind Trotsky decided to visit a Protestant church to see what Christianity was all about. As he arrived for Sunday school, he was received with cold, questioning stares because of his ragged clothes. His heavy accent proved to be even more of a barrier. No one greeted him or said a word to him. They turned their shoulders, cut their eyes, and refused to welcome him.

The Sunday school teacher never arrived, but the lesson was clearly taught, for Trotsky, at least: Christianity is for well-dressed, middle-class white folks. Several years later, he led the Bolshevik Revolution, and the world was never the same. How would Trotsky have been greeted in your church?

Pray that we would greet one another.

Greet one another with an holy kiss. The churches of Christ greet you.

Rom. 16:16

praying for one another

1. Pray that God would open your eyes to the need to warmly welcome people into your church, and into your life.

2. Pray that God would greatly expand your circle of friends and your ability to reach out and develop meaningful relationships.

3. Pray that God would break up power cliques in your church that view visitors as a threat to the status quo.

4. Pray that God would show us how to assimilate new members into the life of the church.

If God is so courteous with us, would it not behoove us to trust one another the same way and "wait for one another"?

Be patient as God works in our lives at different speeds in different ways.

PRAY THAT WE WOULD WAIT FOR ONE ANOTHER
1 Corinthians 11:33

Problems plagued the church at Corinth. They were hopelessly divided into factions ("I am of Paul . . . I am of Cephas . . . I am of Apollos"). There was gross immorality among its members. They were taking one another to court. All this turned out for our benefit. As the apostle addressed each issue in his letter to them, the Holy Spirit inspired him with much practical guidance on how to deal with problems in today's church.

PATIENCE

One of the problems was the riotous and rude way they came together to eat and then to observe the Lord's Supper. Some of the wealthier ones would eat sumptuously while others would watch ravenously. The result was a riotous time of eating, hurt feelings, and a ruined worship experience.

So Paul admonishes them strongly and then concludes with the instruction, "When you come together to eat, *wait for one another*."

Waiting involves patience.

Why is it that when we find ourselves in a group where confession of sin is called for, the one that we are all willing to openly admit is that of impatience, as though this is a "safe sin," not really so bad. Certainly, we think, no one can be faulted for a little impatience.

Yet when Paul begins to describe what *agape* love is all about (1 Cor. 13:4ff), he begins by saying. "Love is patient." The Greek word for patient is that of a slow burn or a long fuse.

Love waits for one another.

When God let His glory pass by Moses, who was hidden in the cleft of the rock, God declared His name and His character, "the Lord God, merciful and gracious, long-suffering." If God is anything, He is patient toward people. Can you even imagine relating to a god who is short suffering? No wonder patience is included among the fruit of the Spirit.

MANNERS

Waiting involves common courtesy.

Max Lucado, in his book *A Love Worth Giving*, points at God's courteousness by reminding us that "Jesus makes Emily Post look like Archie Bunker."

When God comes into our lives, He always brings a gift (the Holy Spirit). He tells us His name (Exod. 3:15) and calls us by ours (John 10:3). He listens to us (Ps. 116:2). He is never early or late, but always right on time. He opens doors for us (2 Cor. 2:12) and offers us a seat with Him in the heavens (Eph. 2:6).

If God is so courteous with us, would it not behoove us to trust one another the same way and "wait for one another"?

Americans are into fast living. We eat at a restaurant not necessarily because it is good food, but because it is fast food. We drive on express-ways in the fast lane. And while we drive, we "multitask" by listening to CDs and talking on our cell phones. A roadside sign spotted recently read, "Right lane, hang up." The best-selling shampoo on the market sells because we can wash and condition in one easy step. There is a funeral home that offers a drive through viewing window for those who don't have time to go inside.

This time frenzy spills over into our churches. We have programs and ministries for every age group and personal need at every possible time on every day of the week. Someone has put it this way:

Mary had a little lamb;
it would have grown to be a sheep.
But it went to all the church events
and died from lack of sleep.

In this time-pressured, stressed-out society, God admonishes us to "wait for one another." Be patient as God works in our lives at different speeds in different ways. Be courteous and kind toward one another as God uses our frustrations with one another to knock off the rough edges of our character in order to conform us to the image of His Son.

Therefore, my brethren,
when you come together to eat,
wait for one another.

1 Cor. 11:33

praying for one another

1. Pray that you will begin to see the interruptions in your daily schedule as divine appointments.

2. Pray that the same spirit of long-suffering that is central to the character of God will become part of your own make-up.

3. Pray that God will reveal to you just how heinous your impatient spirit is and that you might confess it, forsake it, and be delivered from it.

4. Thank God that He is not as impatient with your development and obedience as you are with others.

One way we care for each other is through attentive listening. To feel cared for is to feel listened to.

God blesses churches where members care for one another.

Care equals doing practical things— lawn mowing, car repair, praying.

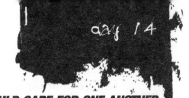

PRAY THAT WE WOULD CARE FOR ONE ANOTHER
1 Corinthians 12:25

WHAT IS A CARING CHURCH?

Imagine this kind of church. Members sue each other before civil courts. Other members habitually attend social banquets honoring strange gods, mere idols. One member lives in open immorality, tolerated by the church. Some think Christian couples ought to separate so they can be more "holy." Worship services are shocking, with some members arriving drunk to partake of the Lord's Supper. Some doubt the validity of Jesus' Resurrection. Many have ceased to give financially.

Who would want to be pastor of this kind of church? Not only was Paul the pastor, but he was the founding pastor, remaining there for eighteen months. To this church in Corinth, Paul wrote, "Care for one another."

The Corinthians were far from caring. This entire chapter is written to comfort those who feel unwanted in church. Have you ever sensed one of these attitudes in your church?

- "If you don't have certain gifts, you're not vital to our church"
- "Our gifts are better than your gifts"
- "Unless you have the gifts we have, you're not yet mature in Christ"

The Greek word for "care" is the same word for "worry" or "anxiety." In this context it means to take concern for; to look after each other's needs; to love or to like; to wish for or to want; to take charge of; to look after; to provide for. One way we care for each other is through attentive listening. To feel cared for is to feel listened to.

CAN YOU HEAR ME NOW?

Here is what a government official by the name of Aristides wrote to the Roman Emperor Hadrian near AD 120 about the Christians of his day:

> They love one another. They never fail to help widows; they save orphans from those who would hurt them. If they have something they give freely to the man who has nothing: if they see a stranger they take him home, and are happy, as though he were a real brother. They don't consider themselves brothers in the usual sense, but brothers instead through the Spirit, in God.

Does this sound like your congregation? Do we make it our business to look after the spiritual, emotional, and physical well-being of each member? Just beneath the surface of our superficial handshakes and plastered smiles are broken hearts or wounded spirits, people and families in crisis.

Anne Ortlund, in her book, *Up with Worship*, describes the church not as a bag of marbles, clicking and clacking against each other, but rather as a bag of grapes, oozing and leaking over one another.

Face it: Ministry is messy. God blesses churches where members care for one another.

Scott Peck wrote in his book *The Road Less Traveled*, "When we love another we give him or her our attention; we attend to that person's growth. . . . By far the most common and important way in which we can exercise our attention is by listening."

In a *Peanuts* cartoon, Charles Schultz had Charlie Brown say, "I wish I could be happy." In the second frame, Charlie says, "I think I could be happy if my life had more purpose to it." In the third frame, Charlie continues, "I also think that if I were happy, I could help others to be happy. Does that make sense to you?" In the fourth frame, Lucy replies, "We've had spaghetti at our house three times this month." To which Charlie Brown replies, "Good grief!"

John McDonald, former head of the U.S. State Department, said, "Americans are known around the world by the inability to listen."

Several members of Wedgwood Baptist Church discovered in the days following the shooting that while fellow church members listened with great sensitivity, others grew weary of our wordage. A few even lost their jobs because they could not or would not stop talking about the shooting. We didn't need advice as much as we just needed to talk. Counselors advised us to talk—and to listen to others as they talked. It was good therapy, but only by those who cared, and listened with love and patience.

Care does not equal curing. How often have you shared a burden with a friend who only made suggestions as to how to cure your problem? They didn't *listen*. They only made suggestions. Care equals *doing* practical things—lawn mowing, car repair, praying.

Mother Teresa was asked, "What are the sources of your strength?" She replied, "A ninety-eight-year-old woman in Philadelphia who prays for me." If we really care for one another, we will faithfully pray for one another.

Pray that we would care for one another.

. . . that there should be no schism,
in the body, but that
the members should have
the same care one for another

1 Cor. 12:25

praying for one another

1. Pray that God would foster a spirit of genuine care and concern for one another in your church.

2. Suggest that your Sunday school class or small study group pass around a prayer request sheet listing the needs and concerns of each member. Make copies for members to pray over throughout the week.

3. Perhaps the church as a whole might make available a list of members' prayer requests.

4. Pray that God will place upon your heart or your family's hearts, several shut-ins or widows that you might personally "adopt" and take care of.

You cannot accept Jesus as Savior and reject Him as Lord.

We either serve one another, or fall into hopeless decay and ruin.

PRAY THAT WE WOULD SERVE ONE ANOTHER
Galatians 5:13

Years ago in a humble Philadelphia hotel, an elderly couple approached the desk clerk. There was a convention in town. All of the hotel rooms were full. Since the clerk was working all night, he offered them his room. The elderly man was John Jacob Astor, who went on to build the famed Waldorf-Astoria Hotel—and hired the young desk clerk, who went on to become one of the greatest hotel men in the world. He *served* and was rewarded for it.

SLAVES TO CHRIST

The theme of Galatians is our freedom in Christ. Judaizers were tempting the church in Galatia to add the legalistic customs of Judaism to the gospel of grace. In other words, one is saved by grace, but still must be circumcised, keep the feast days, and observe other customs. Paul cries out, "Oh, foolish Galatians! Who has bewitched you" (Gal. 3:1)? We are called to freedom!

Chapter five begins with a reference to "freedom in Christ," affirming that believers are not to be "burdened again by the yoke of slavery."

Now that they are called to be "free," they must realize that "freedom in Christ" is not freedom from servanthood. Rather than being common slaves, they are to be uncommon slaves/servants to one another.

Christian freedom involves servanthood. First of all, it involves servanthood to Christ. Jesus said, "Whoever desires to come after Me, let him deny himself and take up his cross and follow Me. For whoever desires to save his life will lose it, but whoever loses his life for My sake and the gospel's will save it" (Mark 8:34-35).

Make no mistake: You cannot accept Jesus as Savior and reject Him as Lord. Salvation involves repentance (forsaking the old, self-centered life) and faith (trust in obedience to Christ). The "allness" of our relationship to Christ is illustrated in an old hymn.

But we never can prove the delights of His love
Until *all* on the altar we lay.
For the favor he shows and this joy he bestows
Are for them who will trust and obey.

SLAVES TO CHRISTIANS

Secondly, Christian freedom involves servanthood to one another.

How can Christians be slaves and be free at the same time?

True freedom in Christ is found through total commitment to Christ. Being a "servant of Christ" means serving one another, perhaps even serving those when no one else is willing to serve.

Christianity Today reported an excellent example of servanthood that was demonstrated following Jim Bakker's release from prison. Two days after his release, a call came to the Salvation Army halfway house where he was living. His request to attend a church service had been met. When he arrived at church, the pastor greeted him warmly and sat him with a family occupying two rows. Just as the organ began playing, the mother of the family entered and sat down next to Jim, proclaiming to the whole world that he was her friend. After the service, Bakker was invited to the family home, where Ruth Graham gave him one of Billy's wallets to replace the prison envelope in which Jim was carrying some addresses.

What is it that hinders us from serving one another?

- *A defeated heart*—the erroneous feeling that there is nothing you can possibly do to be of service to someone else. This is absolutely false. God has both called and equipped every member of the body to a special task or service.
- *A resentful heart*—Perhaps you tried to serve but experienced some criticism. The wrong conclusion is to wallow in self-pity and refuse to try again.
- *A selfish heart*—the lifestyle that insists, "I did it my way! I'm nobody's slave. I'm going to look out for Number One." That kind of spirit is destroying churches across the land.

The story goes of the great violinist, Nicolas Paganini, who donated his marvelous violin to the city of Genoa with the restriction that no one be allowed to play it again. It was agreed upon, and the violin was placed in the town museum for all to see and admire.

But after several decades, the curators were appalled to notice that the wood began to rot and decay. Wood must be handled in order to resist decomposition. Paganini's exquisite violin is now a worm-infested ruin. Life in the body of Christ is like that. We either serve one another, or fall into hopeless decay and ruin.

Pray that we would serve one another.

For you, brethren, have been called to liberty; only do not use liberty as an occasion for the flesh, but by love serve one another.

Gal. 5:13

praying for one another

1. Pray that God would grant you the grace to care for the needs of loved ones and church members without becoming overly anxious and fretful.

2. Pray that God would work in the hearts of your church members to become more transparent and vulnerable enough to share needs with each other.

3. Pray that God would lay upon your heart individuals to whom you can minister specific acts of kindness and ministry.

4. Pray that God might lead your church to organize and fund ministries that are designed to demonstrate care for people in need.

When will we learn that, within and between churches, we are not in competition, but in cooperation?

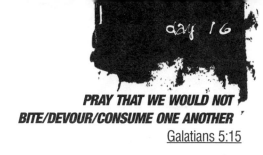

PRAY THAT WE WOULD NOT BITE/DEVOUR/CONSUME ONE ANOTHER
Galatians 5:15

During Oliver Cromwell's rule in England, a serious shortage in coins developed. The order went out to mint new coins, but they found that the only silver in the land was in the statues of the saints in the churches. When the situation was explained to him, Cromwell exhorted, "Well, let's melt down those saints and put them into circulation."

BITE AND DEVOUR

While there is much to be said in favor of believers being put through "melt down" experiences—broken, shaped, molded—this is never to be done in a vicious, vindictive way. To the contrary, we are instructed to avoid such activity when the purpose is to destroy another. Two common Greek verbs often used together in New Testament days to describe the activity of wild animals are translated "bite" and "devour." Not simply "bite," which indicates sudden anger and abuse and the inflicting of pain, but "devour," meaning literally, "to gulp down" or leave no room for anything, which implies continuing in an evil state of mind. Nothing in the text tells us the specific reason for such behavior. It could have been any number of things.

Today we might say they were fighting like cats and dogs. The story goes that two vicious snakes had grabbed each other by the tail and each swallowed the other. The end result was the destruction of both parties involved! Not so common in Bible times was to see sheep biting one another.

CONSUME

The words contain a strong expression of partisan hatred resulting in actions that lead to mutual injury. "Consume" means to spend. It was sometimes used in that day to mean "consumed" as by fire. Used only here and in Luke 9:54, the tense indicates the action has not yet taken place but is potential if conditions continue as is. By "consuming" one another, Paul does not mean that they will lose their status as Christians, but that such activity within the church will eventually destroy the organic community life of the church and eliminate any possibility for Christian fellowship. The more sacred the institution which is disturbed, the more difficult it is to restore harmony. The closer the relationship between wounded individuals, the more difficult it is to restore broken fellowship. The Old

Testament writer of the Proverbs states as much, "A brother offended is harder to win than a strong city" (Prov. 18:19).

COOPERATION

Several years ago at the Special Olympics in Seattle, the one hundred-meter dash had nine entrants. The gun sounded and they all started running as fast as they could. Then one little boy stumbled and fell on the track and began to cry. Hearing him sob, the eight other runners stopped, turned, and looked at him. Seeing him on the ground in tears, everyone abandoned the race and walked back to him. Everyone! One little girl kissed his leg. "There," she said, "that should make it better." Then all nine put their arms around each other and walked together to the finish line to a standing ovation.

When will we learn that, within and between churches, we are not in competition, but in cooperation? When one of us hurts, we all hurt. When one of us advances, the whole kingdom advances.

Of the thousands of letters and calls Wedgwood Baptist Church received after the tragedy, only a paltry few sought to cast guilt or blame. One said the death of these youths was God's punishment for the style of music we were playing. That is what it means to "devour one another."

Thankfully, thousands of churches sent money, gifts, people, and, most of all, heartfelt prayers for healing, grace, protection and provision.

A denominational brochure heralded the annual program theme from Galatians 5:13, "through love serve one another," but inadvertently listed the Scripture as Galatians 5:15. A speaker rose to read the text in a prominent meeting, had everyone turn to Galatians 5:15, and proceeded to read the wrong text, imploring listeners to not "bite and devour one another." If you knew the denomination, you would know how appropriate the mistake was.

Children chant, "Sticks and stones may break my bones, but words will never hurt me." Nothing could be farther from the truth. Words can bite, consume, devour, sting, wreak havoc, and destroy.

Pray that we would not bite/devour/consume one another.

But if you bite and devour one another, take heed that you are not consumed by one another.

Gal. 5:15

praying for one another

1. Pray that a "Kingdom Attitude" seeking the benefit of all God's churches would pervade your heart and that of your church.

2. Call several neighboring churches and ask how you might pray for them.

3. Pray for the well-being of individuals who may have wronged you in the past. Ask God how you might invest in their lives.

4. Do what you can to establish an interdenominational worship service in your community. Begin by sharing with your pastor.

The nature of understanding is linked with a patient spirit towards one another.

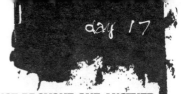

PRAY THAT WE WOULD NOT PROVOKE ONE ANOTHER
Galatians 5:26

There were two classifications of Christians in the Galatian churches. One group believed that they had attained a level of freedom from any restraint whatsoever. They were in danger of turning liberty into license. They were proud of their "freedom." The second group was more timid and scrupulous. The first group would "provoke" the second group to do that which the law forbids, implying that they were afraid to do so. The second group would be prone to "envy" the "freedom" of the first group. (See also Rom. 14:1-15:3 and 1 Cor. 8.)

PROVOKING WITH PRIDE

Having previously discussed the fruit that defines a spirit-filled life, Paul now lists some things that detract from it, one of which is "provoking one another." It indicates an attitude of combat. One translation reads, "challenging one another to rivalry."

One Greek word translates as two or more English words—vain glory or becoming conceited or boasting without basis. This not only leads to pride, but also causes one to provoke another. Such people have a haughty attitude, a holier-than-thou attitude based on the fact that they keep the law better or understand the law better than others. The legalistic attitude evident among many of the Judaizers would breed this kind of mindset. When one bases his life on the keeping of a code of laws, he invariably measures his life by how well he behaves. When he does well, he tends to boast of his accomplishments. This attitude provokes others.

Someone has well said, "Conceit is the only disease that makes everyone sick except the one who has it."

Egotistical pride seems to provoke everyone around us. That is why people loved to hate Muhammad Ali, who blatantly boasted, "I am the greatest."

The story goes that Ali was on an airplane when some turbulence prompted the pilot to flash the "Fasten Your Seatbelt" sign. As the flight attendant asked the champ to comply, he responded truculently, "Hummppff! Superman don't need a seatbelt!" She responded, "Superman doesn't need an airplane, sir, now fasten your seatbelt!"

The world is indeed a better place because Michelangelo never said, "I don't do ceilings" (the Sistine Chapel) or da Vinci did not object to painting church walls ("The Last Supper"). Aren't you glad John Bunyan did not insist on a cash advance before writing *Pilgrim's Progress*? What if William

Carey, the Father of Modern Missions, had insisted on union wages?

What if Jesus hadn't been willing to "humble Himself to the point of death, even the death of the cross" (Phil. 2:8)?

Leonard Bernstein, the famous symphony conductor, was once asked what was the most difficult instrument to play in the orchestra. Without hesitation, he replied, "Second fiddle. I get plenty of first violinists, but to find one who plays second fiddle with as much enthusiasm, or second French horn, or second flute—now that's a problem. And yet, if no one plays second, we have no harmony."

A conceited, vainglorious person is certain to provoke others to dislike and criticize him. It is thus very difficult to preserve brotherly love in a group where one or more persons is puffed up with pride, thinking of themselves more highly than they ought to think (Rom. 12:3).

"Let us not be" is a present middle subjunctive verb in the Greek, meaning "let us cease becoming vainglorious," a word used only here in the New Testament. "Provoking" means "to call forth, to challenge to combat."

UNDERSTANDING WITH PATIENCE

All of us have people in our lives who "rub us the wrong way," irregular people who irritate us. Someone has suggested the first question we will ask when we get to heaven is, "What are YOU doing here?" They may ask the same thing of us!

Proverbs 14:29 states, "He who is slow to wrath has great understanding." The nature of understanding is linked with a patient spirit towards one another.

- Understanding how patient God is with us
- Understanding some of the life experiences that make people peculiar
- Understanding that the Father brings just such people into our lives to knock off the rough edges of our character so that we might better reflect the image of God's Son

If everyone in our congregation were like us in thought, word, and action life would not only be boring, but also our own growth in grace would be stunted.

Pray that we would not become easily provoked and that we would not provoke one another.

Let us not become conceited,
provoking one another,
envying one another.

Gal. 5:26

praying for one another

1. Ask God to show you how to express special thanks to your associate ministers, the church secretary, and custodian. Let them know how you appreciate them.

2. Think of several people in the congregation who have "provoked" you in one way or another. Perform an act of kindness without their knowing who did it.

3. Pray that God would multiply a spirit of humility in your own heart and that of others in your congregation.

4. Pray that God will bless you with "thick skin" and deliver you from being easily hurt.

Envy is the effluvium that oozes from the constant comparison of oneself to others.

Where the fruit of the Spirit is manifested, provocation and envy cannot dwell.

PRAY THAT WE WOULD NOT ENVY ONE ANOTHER
Galatians 5:26

Having discussed the fruit that defines a Spirit-filled life, Paul now lists some things that detract from it, one of which was "provoking one another." The second is "envying one another." "Envying" refers to feelings of jealousy. In the previous chapter, we learned that an epidemic of conceit ("vain glory") in the body results in people "provoking one another." A second result of rampant pride is the equally odious sin of envy.

ENVY AS AN ATTITUDE

Envy is the effluvium that oozes from the constant comparison of one-self to others. Envy was one of the medieval "Seven Deadly Sins," so recognized because they were seminal to a host of subsequent sins. Some of the fruits of envy are backbiting, gossip, slander, bigotry, and vanity.

One is vainglorious when he brags of his situation in life. Such an attitude provokes others. Those who desire to succeed, to be more than they are, are easily irritated by such provocation. The natural response is jealousy, or "envy." Someone who desires to be first cannot stand the success of another.

As persons are provoked, they become envious. Each cannot tolerate the attitude of the other. Nonessentials are treated as matters of life and death and become proof that one is superior to the other. Competition—not motivated by love, the chief fruit of the Spirit—ensues. In fact, attitudes of provocation and envy cause one to lose perspective and balance. Persons lose sight of love, joy, peace, long-suffering, kindness, goodness, faithfulness, gentleness, and self-control and ultimately walk in the flesh, rather than in the Spirit.

Where the fruit of the Spirit is manifested, provocation and envy cannot dwell. A conceited, vainglorious person is liable to be envious of those who receive the attention and respect that he imagines to be due to him.

The Bible has much to say about envy.
- Proverbs 14:30—"envy is rottenness to the bones."
- Proverbs 27:4—"Wrath is cruel and anger a torrent, but who is able to stand before jealousy?"
- Genesis 37:11—It was jealousy that prompted Joseph's brothers to sell him into slavery.
- Matthew 27:18—The Pharisees handed Jesus over "because of envy."

ENVY IN SOCIETY

We live in a competitive society where everyone is striving to "look out for number one." We are a generation that cultivates power lunches and power ties. Mariabelle Stewart, the "Queen of Courtesy," has developed a new seminar to teach the "Manners of Power People." Major "power failures" occur if one should ever violate these edicts:

- Never mash or stir your food.
- Never read the menu carefully. You are not here to eat, but to do business.
- Never, ever hand your plate to the waiter.
- Never stoop down to pick up dropped silverware.

In this society of one-upmanship, envy spills over into our churches. Pastors get caught playing the "Numbers Game." We measure the greatness of a church by the size of its buildings, budget, and busses. Who has the largest choir? The most state-of-the-art computer systems? The most television ads? Or at least the biggest spot in the Yellow Pages?

A spirit of competition and envy causes factions both within churches and between churches. And the only real winner is the devil himself. We become obsessed with inconsequential trivia that serves to divide the body.

How did *she* get the solo in the musical?

Why didn't anyone ask me about the color of the carpet in the nursery?

Why isn't my daughter asked to give her testimony?

Why does his pneumonia merit public prayer and not my gall bladder?

Legend has it that Envy and Greed were walking down a road together when they were confronted by an angel who offered to grant them whatever they desired so long as their companion received twice as much. Finally, Envy spoke up. "I ask that you give me one blind eye." Envy can infiltrate the heart of even the most spiritually mature of us.

The demons were unsuccessfully trying to tempt a holy hermit who lived in the Libyan desert. Try as they might, they could not get him to succumb. Temptations of the flesh, doubts, and fears left him unaffected.

Finally, Lucifer himself was called in. "Your methods are too crude and uncreative," he berated. "Just watch."

Then he whispered into the holy man's ear, "Your brother was just made Bishop of Alexandria."

Slowly, a malignant scowl crept across the hermit's visage.

"Envy," boasted Satan, "is our final weapon against the holiest of saints."

Pray that we would not envy one another.

Let us not become conceited, provoking one another, envying one another.

Gal. 5:26

praying for one another

1. Pray that God would deliver our churches of the spirit of competition and envy.

2. Pray that we might be "plagued" with an epidemic of praise and gratitude for one another both within our churches and between churches.

3. Ask God to show you how you might bless a church other than your own.

4. Pray that God would show you ways you might compliment at least three people every day for the next week. Then do it.

We all sin and thus need to bear
another's burdens that come as
a result of our sins, even as
another bears our burdens.

Only the unconditional acceptance of God
as fleshed out in the body of Christ can
help us bear these crushing burdens.

When someone shares a burden with us,
we are on holy ground and carry a sacred trust.

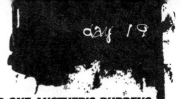

PRAY THAT WE WOULD BEAR ONE ANOTHER'S BURDENS
Galatians 6:2

The passage begins with a man trapped in sin and our need to restore him gently. On the heels of this comes the instruction to "bear one another's burdens." We all sin and thus need to bear another's burdens that come as a result of our sins, even as another bears our burdens. "To bear" means to help or aid another along the way. It refers to the act of carrying a soldier's pack.

WILLINGNESS TO SHARE

Our society and upbringing make it difficult for most of us to let someone else bear our burdens. Do any of these sound familiar?

- "Only the strong survive"
- "Keep a stiff upper lip"
- "Tough it out"
- "When the going gets tough, the tough get going"
- "Big boys don't cry."

At first look, there appears to be a contradiction in the passage. In verse two we are given the command to "bear one another's burden," but in verse five we are told that "each one shall bear his own burden." It is important to note that there are two different Greek words for "burden." In verse five the word is for a normal weight, simply that which can be carried. One need not concern the body with normal, trivial concerns one can carry alone. But in verse two the word for "burden" is that of heavy, crushing, crippling weights. These are too much for any one of us and must be shared to be survived. Some examples of such heavy burdens are

- The burden of loneliness, perhaps the single most debilitating malady of our age. It is crushing the single in his apartment, the teenager who feels misunderstood, the married person whose relationship with his spouse has calcified, the senior citizen who has been passed by in life. Their problems would be bearable if only they did not have to bear them alone.
- The burden of guilt that all of us have experienced. Sins leave scars and wounds that just don't seem to heal. Afraid what others might think, we bear the guilt alone, and it is the devil who loves a secret. Only the people of God have been given the power to relieve tor-

tured souls from the guilt of the past.

- ■ The burden of rejection, experienced by all in some form or another. Parents who were cold and undemonstrative; a critical coach; a girlfriend who dropped you; a spouse who walked out; a boss who promoted someone else.

Only the unconditional acceptance of God as fleshed out in the body of Christ can help us bear these crushing burdens.

LOVING TO BEAR

It is in bearing one another's burdens that we "fulfill the law of Christ." What law is that? In Galatians 5:14 we are told the answer: "For all the law is fulfilled in one word: 'You shall love your neighbor as yourself'". When we genuinely love another, we cannot help bearing one another's burdens.

It is difficult to admit that we have burdens because we fear ridicule. In a cartoon strip, Charlie Brown says, "If I tell you something, Lucy, will you promise not to laugh?"

Lucy responds, "I promise." Charlie Brown continues, "This is very personal, and I don't want you to laugh." Again Lucy replies, "You have my solemn promise." Then Charlie Brown confesses, "Sometimes I lie awake at night listening for a voice that will cry, 'we like you, Charlie Brown.'" "Ha! Ha! Ha! Ha! Ha!" replies Lucy.

In *Why Am I Afraid to Tell You Who I Am*, John Powell says that we are afraid because people might think less of us, might make fun of us and our concerns, might use what they know against us.

Ken Medema painted a picture of the church in song as *the* place for tears to be cried, spirit wings to fly, questions to be asked and our hearts' cries to be heard. When someone shares a burden with us, we are on holy ground and carry a sacred trust. The bottom line is this—we cannot bear one another's burdens if we cannot trust our burdens to each other.

The story is so well known that it has become legendary. Boys Town is a home for orphaned boys near Omaha, Nebraska. During the Depression, two young boys, newly orphaned with nowhere else to go, rode the rails, walked, and hitchhiked their way to the orphanage. Together they braved the elements and the dangers of life on the open road. All they had was each other. As they walked the last several miles, the snow began to fall, and the younger brother began to weaken, so much so that he just could not take another step. So the older boy picked up his younger brother and brought him on his back to the door of the orphanage and knocked. When the priest answered, he asked, "Is there any room for kids like us?"

"Sure, son," replied the priest. "Come on in. Let me take him now. He must be heavy."

"Aw, he ain't heavy, mister. He's my brother."

Pray that we would bear one another's burden.

Bear one another's burdens, and so fulfill the law of Christ.

Gal. 6:2

praying for one another

1. Pray that God would help you become more transparent with those in the body.

2. Pray that God would enable you to see beyond the Sunday morning facades and become aware of people's needs in order to help with their loads.

3. Pray that God would lift the loads of loneliness, guilt, and rejection.

4. Pray that God would send people to your church with a heart and gifts for burden-bearing ministries such as consoling, support groups, and benevolence.

*To bear with each other takes
a deliberate act of the will.
It doesn't happen naturally*

PRAY THAT WE WOULD BEAR WITH ONE ANOTHER

Ephesians 4:2;
Colossians 3:13

We have already seen earlier in Galatians that we are to "bear one another's burdens." This "one another" sounds alike but is different. The earlier word means to assist another with a burden, to carry or lift it. Here "bear" means to be *tolerant* towards other believers to endure patiently their idiosyncrasies and weaknesses to have a forgiving spirit toward others who wrong us.

A FORBEARING SPIRIT

Becoming a Christian doesn't automatically make us lovable. The process of being conformed to Christ's image is just beginning and will take a lifetime of grace. Consequently, there are many in the body of Christ, who fit one writer's description of "irregular people," who tend to rub us the wrong way. With these saints in mind, sometimes we are tempted to sing, "I'm SURPRISED you're a part of the family of God."

Someone has said, "Where there is light, there will be bugs!" The gospel attracts the most wounded and needy of us. That is why God tells us to "bear with one another."

When we refuse to retaliate against believers who have wronged us, when we wait patiently for God to mature immature saints, when we smile and continue to serve the least lovable among us, we are reflecting the very character of our gracious God.

How can this forbearing spirit be expressed towards those in our lives who are hard to bear? The context itself gives us the key.

- We are to relate to others with "all lowliness." Literally, this is a compound word meaning low-mindedness, as opposed to high-mindedness. When Jesus, in the Sermon on the Mount, began by describing the characteristics of a kingdom disciple, the first note he sounded was "poor in spirit." The clearest sign of a believer is a humble spirit that says, "Nothing in my hands I bring; Simply to the cross I cling." When you realize your own spiritual bankruptcy, it is easier to bear with others.
- We are also to relate to others with "gentleness." The King James Version uses the word "meekness." The trouble is, in our society, meekness is associated with weakness. Our Lord described

Himself as "meek and lowly in heart." There was absolutely nothing *weak* about our Savior. What the word implies is a lack of contentiousness, an unwillingness to fight and struggle with God or with others. Why is it that conservative Christians are so noted for their red-faced, acrimonious, looking-for-a-fight attitude?

■ We are to relate to others with "long-suffering," or patience. This word literally means, "having a long fuse, slow to blow up." When God revealed His glorious name and character to Moses on the mount, He included not only mercy and grace, but also long-suffering. It is likewise a part of the fruit of the Spirit. In short, one cannot reflect the image of God without patience. No one of us is perfect. We must be patient with each other. We can't expect more from others than we expect from ourselves. Paul was thankful for the patience the Lord had with him (1 Tim. 1:15-17).

A FORGIVING SPIRIT

Bearing with one another and having a forgiving spirit are synonymous concepts. Colossians 3:13 puts the two together—"bearing with one another, and forgiving one another." Some Christians carry grudges for years. How out of character for a follower of Jesus Christ, who canceled our own debt of sin. Failure to forgive comes in only one flavor—bitter. One day Peter came to Jesus to ask how many times he should forgive his brother? Seven times? Jesus surprised him with seventy times seven. Not 490, but unlimited forgiveness (Matt. 18:21-22). Then Jesus told a parable to show what He meant (Matt. 18:23-35). Author George Herbert once put it this way: "He who cannot forgive another breaks the bridge over which he must pass himself."

Immediately after Paul instructed the Ephesian believers to bear with one another, he said, "endeavoring [making every effort] to keep the unity of the Spirit" (Eph. 4:3). Forbearance does not come naturally; it is not easy. It is what sets genuine believers apart from the rest of humanity because only the power of the Spirit can enable us to bear with one another. To bear with each other takes a deliberate act of the will. It doesn't happen naturally. One chooses to be bitter and unforgiving, and another chooses to be forgiving. Likewise, one must endeavor, make every effort, to keep unity in the body.

Wedgwood Baptist Church is not filled with what the world would call the "movers and shakers" of the city. At present we have no doctors, no politicians. What we do seem to have is a number of blind people, handicapped folks, and special needs children.

One Sunday, a dear woman was having one of her "episodes" where she just runs until she falls. She got up in the middle of the service and ran out. A staff member went running after her and chased her across the baptistery—twice—before catching and restraining her. Throughout it all, the pastor kept preaching.

At times our flesh has cried out, "Oh, God, why don't you send us some of the "Beautiful People"? God continually speaks to our spirit, saying the real test of Wedgwood is how we treat "the least of these" with forbearance, love, and acceptance.

Pray that we would bear with one another.

. . . with all lowliness and gentleness,
with longsuffering,
bearing with one another in love. . . .

Eph. 4:2

praying for one another

1. As you pray, be thankful to God for all the old sins already forgiven in you, and thereby develop a grateful, forbearing spirit.

2. Ask God to let you see all of your fellow believers with godly eyes—hurting, wounded, broken, in-need-of-grace believers.

3. Ask God to reveal to you any smoldering resentment of past hurts and wrongs and to heal you of the poison left in your soul.

4. Thank God for the people in your life who have been patiently forbearing as you have gone through the process of becoming more like Christ.

*Kindness in our churches not only
sympathizes with the needy and
hurting, but also it seeks to
relieve the hurt and meet the need.*

PRAY THAT WE WOULD BE KIND TO ONE ANOTHER
Ephesians 4:32

In a school classroom, the teacher gave an essay assignment. The students were to look at the famous piece of art, "The Spirit of '76." You may remember it. Three men are marching, one with a drum, one with a fife, and one with a bandage around his head. One boy wrote: "'The Spirit of '76' is a painting of three men. One of them is beating a drum; one of them is blowing a horn; and the other one has a headache."

BECOMING KIND

In this day of much drum beating and horn blowing, we need to be kind, tenderhearted, and forgiving. One of the first verses many of us learned was, "Be kind to one another." The verse literally says, "Become kind," suggesting that it may be a matter of growth and attainment. We are not kind by nature. We must become kind.

"Kind" means "full of benign courtesy" "the disposition of mind which thinks as much of its neighbor as it does of its own" "thoughtful consideration." Kindness looks outward, not inward. "Tenderhearted" connotes compassion and warm sympathetic love. "Forgiving" speaks of grace, and is built on the same word as grace—unmerited favor.

We are to offer undeserved forgiveness, just as we are undeserving of Jesus' forgiveness toward us. Forgive as in the parable of the two debtors (Luke 7:32).

In one sentence, Paul lays down the law of personal relationships. Treat others as Jesus has treated us. The Greek word for kindness carries an added dimension that the English does not convey. It means not only gracious and pleasant, but there is an element of usefulness as well. As Max Lucado relates in his book *A Love Worth Giving*, kindness is both pleasant and practical. Jesus not only attended the wedding at Cana, He salvaged it. He did more than acknowledge Zacchaeus. He blessed him with His presence in his home.

Kindness in our churches not only sympathizes with the needy and hurting, but also it seeks to relieve the hurt and meet the need. Kindness not only opens the door for the elderly, but also it makes sure the church is handicapped accessible. Kindness not only smiles at the toddlers, but also it makes sure that the rooms are environmentally safe and that policies are in place to protect them from predators. Kindness not only prays for the sick, but also it provides rubber gloves for nursery workers, policies for disease control, and health insurance for staff members.

KINDNESS AS RESPECT

In the aftermath of the shooting at Wedgwood Baptist Church, our church was treated with respect and courtesy by the press. As far as we know, not a single adverse article or interview came out in the media. This seemed so contrary to what so many others have experienced with what seems to be an anti-Christian bias in the media.

We believe the difference was that God led us, in the midst of our grief and shock, to treat the press with respect and kindness. As the pastor was waiting to be interviewed on one of the major networks, he heard one of the commentators say that they had received e-mails and calls criticizing the media for making a living off other people's tragedies. We thought, how unfair to "shoot the messenger." Our nation depends on a free and active press.

Reporters and interviewers universally offered their services to us. "If there's anything we can do, please let us know." So after the interview, the pastor asked for a favor. "Sure! Anything!" He asked if they would allow him to pray for them. Then they joined hands—the interviewers, the soundmen, the cameramen, and the pastor—and he prayed for them.

He asked God to protect them from harm and temptation while they were away from their families. He asked God to protect them from editors who would twist the truth of their interview into misleading sound bites. And he prayed that they would come to know Christ, who gave us hope in our hour of need. When he finished, many were wiping tears. All expressed their gratitude. And no one bashed us. All it took was a little kindness.

Pray that we would be kind to one another.

And be kind to one another,
tenderhearted, forgiving one another,
just as God in Christ has forgiven you.

Eph. 4:32

praying for one another

1. Pray that God would increase your kindness quotient toward the members of your church and toward the lost.

2. Ask God to show you specific people for whom you might show love and kindness—both gracious courtesy and practical usefulness.

3. Pray that God would open the eyes of your church for systemic changes that convey an attitude of kindness to others.

4. Spend time alone recalling all the various acts of kindness others have shown to you and then give God thanks.

> *The concept of submission is central to Christianity. One enters the kingdom by faith in and submission to Jesus Christ.*

> *God, give us churches where Christ is in charge and people are in the habit of submitting to one another.*

PRAY THAT WE WOULD SUBMIT TO ONE ANOTHER
Ephesians 5:21;
I Peter 5:5

SUBMISSION AS OBEDIENCE

Ask most Christians what they think of when they hear the word "submission," and they will respond with something about marriage. One reason for this response is that the Bible does speak of wifely submission (Eph. 5:22; Col. 3:18; Titus 2:5; 1 Pet. 3:1).

However, the word has a larger meaning. "Submission" is a synonym for "obedience." It means to yield to another's admonition and advice.

- Young men were to be submissive to older men (1 Pet. 5:5).
- All members of the body were to submit to authority (Heb. 13:17).
- Servants were to submit to masters (Titus 2:9; Eph. 6:5; Col. 3:22; 1 Pet. 2:18).
- Children were to submit to parents (Eph. 6:1; Col. 3:20).
- Citizens were to submit to government leaders (Rom. 13:1; 1 Pet. 2:13). Paul is simply echoing Jesus' words in Matthew 20:25-28 and matching the description of Jesus in Philippians 2:6-7.

The word originally arose from military usage in the Apostle Paul's day. It literally meant "to rank under," to be subordinate to someone.

The concept of submission is central to Christianity. One enters the kingdom by faith in and submission to Jesus Christ. Jesus Himself was astounded that anyone would dare to call Him "Lord" and refuse to obey His word (Luke 6:46). Later, when Roman persecution came, everyone was called to publicly confess, "*Kurios Caesar!*" ("Caesar is lord!"). True believers refused, proclaiming instead, "*Kurios Jesu!*" ("Jesus is Lord!"), and they paid for their submission to Christ with their very lives.

MUTUAL SUBMISSION

Mutual submission is uniquely Christian. Others operate out of selfish motives. When mutual submission is lacking in a church—look out. Fights and splits occur because both sides of a disagreement want their own way and neither will submit.

Submission is the ability to lay down the burden of always needing to get our own way. To borrow a phrase from the game of poker, you've got to know when to hold 'em and know when to fold 'em.

Early in the fifth century, a controversy over the nature of Christ was tearing the church apart. The two main opponents were Cyril, Bishop of Alexandria, and Nestorius, Bishop of Constantinople. The division grew so sharp that the Emperor was led to call the Third Ecumenical Council in AD 431 to settle the issue. Cyril and his supporters arrived first and, without waiting for the others to arrive, they convened, elected Cyril president, denounced Nestorius as a heretic, and stirred up the populace against him and his followers. Forced to reconvene, Nestorius and his followers claimed to be the legitimate council and condemned Cyril and his disciples as heretics. When they both appealed to the Emperor, he condemned them all. The result was a divided, broken, embittered church.

This sad story has been repeated again and again abroad as well as on a local scale. It is well known that the main factor in church starts is division in existing churches. When New Harmony Church sets up shop just down the road from Old Harmony Church, one can be sure there has been precious little harmony among the brethren.

What is needed is a fresh understanding of what it means to "submit to one another."

Submission does not mean inequality between persons. Galatians 3:28 clearly tells us that all of us—Jews and Greeks, males and females, slave and free man—are equal as persons in the eyes of Christ. Someone has well said, "The ground is level at the foot of the cross."

Nor does submission mean inferiority of role. Wives are just as critical to a godly home as are their husbands; the President's vote counts no more than the average citizen's. Jesus said, "I do always the will of my Father," yet He, as the second Person of the Trinity, is no less God than the Father Himself.

Submission is merely the subjugation of one's will for the sake of the whole. A young man decided to muster out of the Marine Corps after ten years of service. A few weeks later he came back and re-enlisted. As he explained, "Sarge, no one is in charge out there!"

God, give us churches where Christ is in charge and people are in the habit of submitting to one another.

Pray that we would submit to one another.

. . . submitting to one another
in the fear of God.

Eph. 5:21

praying for one another

1. Pray that God will reveal to you which issues in your faith and practice are negotiable and which are not.

2. Pray that a spirit of mutual submission would spread in your congregation.

3. Pray that your family members would come to know the joy of submitting to one another.

4. Pray that our homes and churches become crucibles for mutual submission rather than battlegrounds of egos.

*The most deadly lies of all,
however, are the lies we live.*

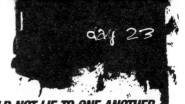

PRAY THAT WE WOULD NOT LIE TO ONE ANOTHER
Colossians 3:9

Paul may have singled out the sin of lying for special treatment because in it, more than in any other sin, we demonstrate ill will toward one another. The verb is present imperative, which combined with the negative, forbids the continuation of the act. So some translations word this, "Stop lying!" or "Do not continue the habit of lying."

PUTTING OFF LYING

When we "put off the old man" and "put on the new man," we should be done with lying, since lying is clearly not a part of the new nature. Lying is listed in verse eight—with the things that we must "put off"—used in the sense of putting off clothes.

When a new believer was baptized in the New Testament, he took off his old robe, and after coming up out of the water, put on a new robe. It was a part of the symbolism of new life in Christ.

Do you remember the story of Pinocchio, the wooden puppet who was miraculously changed into a living boy? The childless puppet maker was overjoyed! But there was one fatal flaw in the lad: He could not stop lying. Each lie would cause his nose to grow a little longer. One lie would lead to another. It was Sir Walter Scott who said, "Oh, what a tangled web we weave/when first we practice to deceive."

Our first President was supposedly known for his truthfulness ("I cannot tell a lie"). Modern politicians are known for their unreliability ("I misspoke!"). We have become a nation of liars. We cheat on tests at school, plagiarize papers, falsify tax returns, and create sparkling resumes from nothing. According to the Institute of American Behavior, ninety-one percent of us lie at least three times a day.

We are guilty when we tell bold untruths to one another. From the laws of Moses to the Code of Hammurabi, a false witness was considered to be an egregious sin. From the thoughts of Greek philosophers to the ideas of Roman senators, lying lips were abhorrent. Proverbs 12:22 says, "Lying lips are an abomination to the Lord." Nothing could be more contrary to God who is truth personified.

LYING IN GOSSIP

But we are also guilty when we are involved in slander and gossip with each other. Psalm 15:2-3 says he who truly worships, "speaks the truth in his heart . . . does not backbite with his tongue . . . nor does he take up a reproach against his friend."

Someone has well said, "The only reason a gossip likes to *talk* so much is that we like to *listen* to it so well." The most popular sport in many churches is "jumping to conclusions."

But we are also guilty of falsehood when we break our contracts. We have read of athletes who refuse to play for "chump change" ($500,000 a year) and walk out on their contracts. But every week churches languish because of volunteers who fail to show up for duty that they agreed to perform.

LYING IN SILENCE

Lastly, we lie to one another when we slink in cowardly silence rather than boldly speak the truth people do not want to hear. To say nothing when lies are being propagated is tantamount to agreement. The German pastor Martin Niemöller confessed, "When they came for the Negroes, I said nothing. When they came for the Communists, I said nothing. When they came for the Jews, I said nothing. Now that they have come for me, there is no one left to raise their voice in protest."

The most deadly lies of all, however, are the lies we live. Many have pretended for so long to be something they are not, and they are unaware of the real truth. They are like the Chinaman who was hired to play the flute in the Emperor's orchestra—when he couldn't play a note! For years he held the instrument to his lips and faked it. Then one day the Emperor decided he wanted to hear a solo from each man in the orchestra. As the fateful day approached, he became more and more distraught. Finally, on the morning of his own recital, he drank poison and committed suicide. The Chinese say he was "afraid to face the music."

Our words ought to be fountains of consolation, illumination, and encouragement, yet they are more often floods of untruths and half-truths that sting and bite like serpents. If all the talk that has its source in lies were suddenly made inaudible, what a deadly silence would fall on many a church gathering. Some who sing would be lip-syncing. Some who pray in public would be leading in silent prayer. Even some who preach would have gaps of wordless content in their sermon illustrations. Many would stand with lips moving, but no words coming out of their mouths.

Pray that we would not lie to one another.

Do not lie to one another,
seeing that you have put off
the old man with his deeds. . . .

Col. 3:9

praying for one another

1. Pray for God to reveal and expunge every falsehood in your own life.

2. Pray that God will deliver you from the desire to hear information about others that should not be reported.

3. Pray that God will bless your congregation with transparent lives among its members.

4. Pray that you and your believing friends would be bold in speaking the truth in love.

God doesn't expect us to refrain from grief or mourning, but to "sorrow not as others who have no hope."

The worst this old world can do to us is kill us, and that only ushers us into the presence of the Lord in glory.

PRAY THAT WE WOULD COMFORT ONE ANOTHER
1 Thessalonians 4:18

WHEN WILL JESUS RETURN?

The church in Thessalonica was becoming increasingly discouraged. They were all first-generation believers and lived with the strong conviction that they would see the return of Jesus. Each day they arose with the eager expectation, "Perhaps today."

But the Lord delayed His return (and still does). Worse still, these new Christians had suffered the grief of seeing friends and loved ones slip over the brink of eternity as life and death took its natural toll. What about those who have died ("asleep")? When Christ returns, what will happen to them?

So Paul wrote his first epistle to them to give them hope and comfort in the face of the last enemy to be defeated—death itself. Paul does not tell them to stop their grieving.

Those who would short-circuit the natural, God-given process of working through our sorrow by some sort of Pollyanna denial, end up with far more emotional and physical problems. The God who created our tear ducts encouraged us to "weep with those who weep." God doesn't expect us to refrain from grief or mourning, but to "sorrow not as others who have no hope."

Then Paul explains the basis of our "blessed hope." Christ *will* return. When He does, the bodies of those who have died will rise incorruptible. We who are alive and remain shall be "caught up together with them in the clouds to meet the Lord in the air." It will be glorious; it will be forever. No more good-byes.

"Therefore," Paul says, "comfort one another with these words." He would repeat these words in 1 Thessalonians 5:11, adding the admonition to "encourage one another."

These words are not just soft, vacuous cooing or whistling in the dark. The believer's hope is rooted in the historic fact of the resurrection of Jesus Christ. Because He lives, we too shall live. He conquered death and hell to demonstrate that the grave no longer has a hold on those who live and believe on Him (John 11:25, 26).

JESUS WENT FIRST

As children, we loved to challenge each other to daring feats. Who would be the first one to jump in the river in the spring? Who would take the challenge to dive off the high dive at the city park? Who would dare to go down the slide standing up? Somehow, it was always easier to do anything if someone else did it first (and lived to tell about it).

Jesus drank the bitter dregs of Calvary's cup and descended into the grave, where He remained for three days. Then, on that first resurrection morn, He broke the shackles of sin and death and ascended to glory. Thus the grave was robbed of its victory; death was stripped of its sting. The worst this old world can do to us is kill us, and that only ushers us into the presence of the Lord in glory.

We live in a society that longs to hear, "It's OK." We long for comfort and hope. But for those who know not Christ, it will *not* be OK—forever.

However, for the body of Christ, an old hymn says it best: "Earth has no sorrow that Heaven cannot heal." And no matter how good things may get, the best is yet to come. What comfort!

The tragic shooting at Wedgwood Baptist Church occurred only two days after the funeral of the pastor's mother. As therapy for processing this grief as well as that for his mother, a counselor instructed him to return to his childhood home in Michigan. There he walked from empty room to empty room, haunted by the sounds of laughter and tears, good memories and bad. He bade his mother and father "good-bye" and began to weep at the sense of their loss. An old Isaac Watts hymn flooded his mind:

> When I can read my title clear
> To mansions in the skies.
> I'll bid farewell to every tear
> And wipe my weeping eyes.

He was smothered by the sense of loss, not only of parents, but also of the seven young people who were murdered in our sanctuary. Grieving, he sang on:

> Let cares like a wild deluge come
> And storms of sorrow fall

Then he broke down into sobs. "They've come, Lord. Such a Storm of Sorrow! How will we ever bear it all?" he asked God. And then the last line came:

> May I but safely reach my home
> My God, my heaven, my all.

God, in His infinite mercy, sent waves of comfort through poetic words of encouragement written centuries before, having their root in the eternal promises of God.

Pray that we would comfort one another.

*Therefore comfort one another
with these words.*

1 Thess. 4:18

praying for one another

1. Take time to meditate on the joyous greeting you will receive in heaven from loved ones who have gone on before. Best of all, envision the Lord Himself with open arms saying, "Well done." Take comfort.

2. Do you know of someone needing comfort? What could you do in the next few days to comfort them?

3. Do you know of someone who is confused over the events of the end times? Why not replace their confusion with comfort?

4. Pray for comfort for the families of those listed in today's obituaries.

*It's hard to function, especially
in the body of Christ without
the encouragement of others.*

*Affirm others for who they are,
not for who you want them to be.*

PRAY THAT WE WOULD EDIFY ONE ANOTHER
1 Thessalonians 5:11

At the Pacific Ocean Studios on Clement Street in San Francisco, there is a pipe organ called the Chamberlain Music Master. What is distinctive about this organ is that there is a special button that, when pushed, offers a round of concert hall sized applause. You can play anything, press the button, and get a virtual standing ovation. Who would not enjoy the affirmation of a standing ovation to life's experiences? It's hard to function, especially in the body of Christ without the encouragement of others.

BUILDING UP CHARACTER

The earlier Greek verb in this verse renders the same Greek verb as the word "comfort" in 1 Thessalonians 4:18. Then Paul used another Greek verb, translated "edify" which means applaud/build up/encourage. The readers were not being asked to do something new. Paul mentions that this comforting and edifying is something "you also are doing." This, then, is an encouragement to continue what they have already been practicing.

This verb and its corresponding noun (edification) occur more than twenty-five times in the New Testament, usually in the writings of Paul. Paul uses it each time in a social context, referring to interpersonal relationships within the church and the growth of the body. To edify one another, as Paul here uses the word, means to assist another in the building up of character.

Various philosophers and theologians have used the terms "basement people" and "balcony people" to describe the two types of people in our lives. Basement people control us. They say things like: "You can't do that" "That's a stupid thing to do" "When will you ever get it right?" They divert our hopes and dreams by constantly pointing out the negative things in our lives. They cause the room to light up when they leave. Balcony people are full of love and cheer us on to be loving and courageous when we are tempted to give up. They sit in the balcony of our lives and cheer us on. They say things like: "You can do it" "Go for it" "Seize the moment."

We are called to be balcony people who encourage one another. Our hero in this activity is Barnabas. His name means "son of encouragement" (Acts 4:36). Barnabas stood up for Paul when no one else did (Acts 9:26-31). He stood up for Mark when Paul did not.

Would you like to be an encourager in your church or fellowship group? Here are some practical suggestions for encouragement:

- Be vocal in encouraging others
- Affirm others for who they are, not for who you want them to be
- Allow others to be your balcony people
- Encourage those who are overlooked by others

NECESSITY OF ENCOURAGING

One of the business marvels of the past twenty-five years has been the rise and dominance of Wal-Mart stores as America's number-one retailer. One of the essential secrets of Wal-Mart's growth has been its policy and practice of friendly management.

There is a grandpa- or grandma-like greeter at every front door with a smile and an offer to help. There is the "ten-foot policy," which requires every employee who comes within ten feet of a customer to smile, greet, and offer assistance.

Every employee, from the late Sam Walton himself to the stock boy, is on a first-name basis. Wal-Mart realizes the necessity of encouraging one another.

Wes Seeliger writes, "Ever feel like a frog? Frogs feel slow, low, ugly, puffy, drooped, pooped. The frog feeling comes when you want to be bright, but feel dull; when you want to share, but feel selfish; you want to be thankful, but feel resentment; you want to be big, but you are small; you want to care, but you are indifferent. We've all had times when we felt like a frog, floating on a lily pad down the great river of life, too froggish to budge.

Once upon a time, there was a frog. But he really wasn't a frog. He was a prince who looked and felt like a frog. A wicked witch had cast a spell on him. Only the kiss of a beautiful young maiden could save him. So he sat— an unkissed prince in frog form.

But miracles happen. One day a beautiful maiden grabbed him up and gave him a big smack. Crash! Boom! Zap! There he was—a handsome prince. And you know the rest of the story. They lived happily ever after.

So what is the task of the church? To kiss frogs, of course!"

Pray that we would edify and encourage one another.

Therefore comfort each other
and edify one another,
just as you also are doing.

1 Thess. 5:11

praying for one another

1. Ask God to open your eyes to church members and Christian friends who could use a word of encouragement.

2. Send birthday cards to the senior adults in your congregation. Perhaps the church secretary or seniors minister can get the information for you.

3. Seek to be a Barnabas ("son of encouragement"), trying to compliment and affirm at least one person every day.

4. Find someone who can be an encourager to you, and allow them to build you up in the faith.

*If the church is anything at all,
it should be stimulating–never boring.*

*The common term "inactive church member"
is an oxymoron, internally contradictive;
like a blazing snowball, or a square circle.*

PRAY THAT WE WOULD CONSIDER ONE ANOTHER
Hebrews 10:24

In the wake of the Wedgwood shooting, there was a real need for church members to push each other along through the crisis—not back to the old norm, but to a new norm.

CONSIDERATION

The Greek word used here literally means not only "to consider one another" but also to consider and care for one another in order to exhort or spur them on, to stimulate them. Even though verse 25 says, "exhort one another," this is not the same Greek word—*allelon* translated "one another" in our study. So, more fully translated, the verse would read: "Consider one another to exhort them to love and good works." The purpose of the consideration was to "exhort," or stimulate.

We don't take the time to consider one another. We live in an increasingly isolated and lonely world. We shop through the Internet; we get our money from an ATM machine; we purchase our food in a drive-through restaurant, where all we see are the impersonal hands of someone handing us our burgers. In Virginia there is a funeral home where one can drive through, pause at the window (supposedly commenting on how "natural" the body looks), and then drive on without ever having to get out of the car.

We live in neighborhoods without sidewalks, with our garage in the back, surrounded by a privacy fence, but no front porch. These are our moats. Our homes are modern medieval castles! The by-word of our age is, "Mind your own business!"

That is why the local church is the hope of the world! We are a body living in relationship with each other. Today's verse commands us to "consider one another." Literally, it means to stare through and take careful, continuous care of one another; look after one another.

Wives "consider" husbands. They are constantly looking after and caring for us. They see that our clothes are clean and neat. They are more concerned about what we eat than we are—trying to disguise broccoli and spinach in delicious casseroles. While such consideration is hopefully rooted in love, it also stimulates love.

STIMULATION

The text urges us to "stir up" (stimulate) love and good works in each other. If the church is anything at all, it should be stimulating—never boring. Robert Louis Stevenson once wrote in his journal: "Went to church today—was not greatly depressed." What an indictment! Church should never be mediocre and dull, and neither should Christians.

We should provoke folks to love. Some would object: "You cannot make people love you." Of course you can! Love and care are so rare these days that even your worst enemies are so desperate for it they'll shed their animosity to get it. As Edwin Markham wrote:

> He drew a circle that shut me out
> Heretic, rebel, a thing to flout.
> But love and I had the wit to win
> We drew a circle and shut him in!

You can also stimulate folks to good works. Any behavior modification teacher will tell you, when folks mess up at nothing or when they do good, shower them with praise. Bring out the best in one another.

We should consider one another in order to exhort each to find his ministry within his own personality. Abraham was a wanderer, an adventurer. God called him to travel to an unknown place. One woman was exhorted by her pastor to find her ministry. She decided her best asset was her smile, so she arrived early and stayed late each Sunday to smile people in and out of the church services. Another lady was exhorted to minister to lonely students at a nearby university, so she made index cards for the bulletin boards with invitations for tea and cookies at 4:00 p.m. each day in her home. At her funeral several years later, she had eighty pallbearers, all lonely students who had found a friend who ministered to them.

As you exhort others ask them three questions, and their ministry will likely come out of one of the answers:

- What tugs at your heart?
- What do you like to do?
- What are you good at doing?

The author of Hebrews goes on to give a negative illustration: "not forsaking the assembling of ourselves together" (Heb. 10:25). The common term "inactive church member" is an oxymoron, internally contradictive; like a blazing snowball, or a square circle. To be a member of a church is, by definition, to be active in the body, stimulating each other to love and to good works.

Pray that we would consider one another.

And let us consider one another so as to stir up love and good works. . . .

Heb. 10:24

praying for one another

1. Pray that God will reveal your own spiritual gifts and then have you serve.

2. Pray that God will show you how to care for folks, especially family friends and church members.

3. Pray that God will send a spirit of care and concern for the members of your church.

4. Ask God to reveal what specific act of kindness you might do to stimulate someone to love and good works.

We may have differences between each other, but we are never to attack one another.

PRAY THAT WE WOULD NOT SPEAK EVIL OF ONE ANOTHER
James 4:11

LOOSE LIPS

During World War II a poster displayed throughout American defense plants cryptically read, "Loose lips sink ships." The point was that idle talk about defense production could give vital information to the enemy.

Whether the church realizes it or not, we are in the conflict of the ages. The foes of darkness have sworn to snuff out the light of life. Sadly, our forces are plagued with loose lips, gossiping tongues, and saints who destroy one another by speaking evil of one another.

James begins this chapter by talking of wars and fights among the brethren, and then goes on to point out the absolute necessity of humility before God. Backbiting and gossip are subtle forms of self-exaltation. The premise goes: "If I can put you down, that makes me look better."

But God commands us "not to speak evil of one another." Some people make it their life's calling to be the bearer of bad news. The first section they turn to in the newspaper is the legal section. Who is suing whom? Who is getting divorced? Who is going bankrupt? Who has run afoul of the law today? Then they hurry on down to their favorite coffee shop to share the gory details with their fellow assassins.

In Proverbs 6:16-19, God lists seven things that He hates. Among these are "a lying tongue . . . a false witness . . . and one who sows discord among brethren." All of these fall under the category of "speaking evil of one another."

Why are Christians the only army that tortures its own wounded? When a brother has fallen, we kick the sick; we knock those in shock!

God says, "Don't do it! Cut that out!"

"But it's true," we object. The truth or falsehood of the matter is not the issue. Someone has well said that you can be sure it is gossip if the one you are talking to is neither the cause nor the solution to the problem.

God, in grace, gave us two reasons we should not speak evil of one another. First, we are *family*. Three times in verse 11, we find the word, "brother." We may have differences between each other, but we are never to attack one another. That is an act of self-mutilation. When one part of the body hurts, we all hurt.

LOOSE HEARTS

The second reason we should not speak evil of one another has to do with

119

presumption. To speak evil of a brother positions us above the law. Which law? The royal law found in James 2:8: "Love your neighbor as yourself."

John Wesley and George Whitefield led the Evangelical Awakening in the eighteenth century. Because of theological differences the followers of these two men were often at war with each other in splits and arguments. Once a reporter asked Wesley if he expected to see Whitefield in Heaven.

Wesley replied, "No, I do not." Then he explained why. "George Whitefield is such a godly man, I expect he will be among the inner circle right next to the throne of God. I will be so far back among the throng, I probably won't even be able to *see* Whitefield."

During the tragedy in Wedgwood Baptist Church, the shooter was heard cursing and denouncing Baptists. In the aftermath, we discovered that his family had been active in another denomination for generations. It would have been easy to make it a holy war, but God gave grace for us to realize that this senseless event had nothing to do with denominational convictions. In fact, a neighboring church of his denomination has become very dear to our congregation and shown love to us in many ways. We have found, indeed that: "Blest be the tie that binds our hearts in Christian love."

One woman came to her pastor to beg forgiveness of him. It seems she had been spreading vicious rumors about him throughout the town. Now under conviction from God, she begged his pardon. The pastor retreated into the back of the house and came back with a pillow. He then took a knife and slashed the pillow open. The wind caught the feathers and soon spread them across the neighborhood. "I will forgive you," he said, "when you return with every feather."

"Oh! How could I ever do that?" she cried. "They're spread all over town."

The pastor replied, "So too is the damage done to me by these lies you've repeated."

We can be forgiven for speaking evil of one another, but eternity alone can heal the damage.

A four-year-old tried to recite the Lord's Prayer: "And forgive us our trash-baskets as we forgive those who trash basket against us."

Pray that we would not speak evil of one another.

Do not speak evil of one of another,
brethren. He who speaks evil
of a brother, and judges his brother,
speaks evil of the law, and judges the law.
But if you judge the law, you are not
a doer of the law but a judge.

Jas. 4:11

praying for one another

1. Pray for an end to gossip and backbiting within congregations and denominations.

2. Pray that a familial sense of brotherhood will abound across the kingdom.

3. The next time you are called upon to pray in public, ask for God's spiritual blessing to fall on other churches. Name them specifically.

4. Ask God to give you grace to never again publicly disagree with or dispute with another member of the family of God.

Believers are encouraged to show stamina without grumbling.

PRAY THAT WE WOULD NOT GRUMBLE AGAINST ONE ANOTHER
James 5:9

JESUS IS THE JUDGE

The readers of James' letter were victims of mistreatment by the wealthy (Jas. 5:1-6). Such trials often produce grumbling or complaining. James writes to encourage them to "not grumble," but rather be patient. Believers are encouraged to show stamina without grumbling. The literal meaning of the Greek word translated in most English translations as "grumble" is "to groan" or "to sigh heavily." It reflects an inward, unexpressed feeling of sorrow created by undesirable circumstances. Mark uses this word for Jesus in Mark 7:34. Paul uses it for believers in Romans 8:23 and again in 2 Corinthians 5:2, 4. There is no room for this in the family of God.

The reason for not grumbling is "lest you be condemned." We are to treat one another in such a way that you will not need Jesus to act as a Judge, and the Judge is already at the door. Blaming another, condemning another, often leads to condemnation upon self.

The context of this encouragement is a discussion on patience with three illustrations. The first is of the farmer who patiently waits for his land to produce crops. He must prepare the soil, and then sow the seed during the time of the "early rain" toward the end of October. Then the farmer has to keep the fields free of weeds, being patient, and trust God for a harvest just after the "latter rain" in late April or early May. So, too, they were to be patient, not grumbling, because the return of the Lord was near.

Grumbling prevents us from developing patience. Instead it develops a critical spirit and a faultfinding lifestyle. Sometimes we even blame our predicament on others.

JESUS WILL RETURN

While the lesson is one of patience, the reason James gives for not grumbling is the imminent return of Jesus. They lived as though Jesus were returning at any moment. The New Testament urges us so to live. They were only a few years away from the days in which Jesus promised His followers that He would return, and yet they were grumbling. We are two thousand years removed from His prediction, and we likewise grumble. Regardless of the age in which one lives, grumbling is forbidden in light of the sure return of Jesus.

The story goes of a man who entered a monastery sworn to the discipline of silence. Each monk was allowed only two words every ten years.

After ten years of silence, each monk was called in to confer with his abbot in his customary two-word dialogue.

The abbot asked him, "After ten years among us, what you would like to say?"

"Food bad," the monk replied. Then he went back to his cell.

Ten years later, he was called in again. This time he said, "Bed hard," and returned to his contemplation.

Finally, after thirty years, he was called in for a third interview. With exasperation, he said, "I quit!"

"It doesn't surprise me at all," said the abbot. "You've done nothing but complain around here for thirty years."

Grumbling and complaining are not spiritual gifts, contrary to what some might claim. They are habits that drain the body of joy. Remember how the grumbles among the people of God brought death and disaster in the wilderness? A whole generation of grumblers had to be buried in the desert before the Israelites could possess the land.

This doesn't mean we should not address situations that need correction. But be tactful when you express your concern.

In a country church in Croatia at the beginning of the twentieth century, an altar boy named Josep Broz served the priest at Sunday mass. Nervous and fearful, he dropped the cup. Angrily, the priest slapped the boy and shouted, "Leave, and do not come back!" He never did. That boy became known as Tito, the Communist leader of Yugoslavia.

About the same time in Peoria, Illinois, another altar boy named Peter John also dropped the cup at mass. Instead of grumbling and condemning, the bishop smiled and gently whispered, "Someday you will be just what I am." That boy grew up to be Archbishop Fulton J. Sheen, one of the most eloquent spokesmen for the Roman Catholic Church.

We are like students fighting in a teacherless classroom as the teacher is returning from a visit to the office. We are like workers fighting in a supervisorless work place while the supervisor is returning from a conference with the boss. We are like children fighting in a parentless room while the parent is returning from responsibilities in another room. Don't grumble. The Lord's return is at hand.

Pray that we would not grumble against one another.

Do not grumble against one another,
brethren, lest you be condemned.
Behold, the judge is standing at the door!

Jas. 5:9

praying for one another

1. Pray that God Himself will control your tongue each day.

2. Pray that God will give you a heart to see and applaud what is good rather than notice and complain about what is bad.

3. Ask God to reveal all the wounds you have received through other's complaints and pray for deep, permanent healing.

4. Pray for an epidemic of joyful gratitude in your congregation.

There are obvious benefits to confession. The process allows us to experience God's forgiveness.

Whatever shame and revulsion we might experience as we publicly confess under the Holy Spirit pales in comparison to the blessings received when we are obedient.

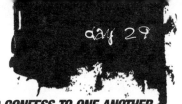

PRAY THAT WE WOULD CONFESS TO ONE ANOTHER
James 5:16

The Greek word for "confess" means literally to "say again" or "agree with." So when we confess our sins, we are saying the same thing God says about them, rather than using our own euphemistic descriptions. What we might excuse as righteous indignation God calls an angry attitude. What we might call fearful sensitivity, God calls a man-pleasing spirit. We are to stop making excuses, or casting blame, or rationalizing, and take responsibility for our sins. What do you think God is saying about your sin?

CONFESS TO WHOM?

Some believe that in order to receive forgiveness, confession must be made before a priest. Most Evangelicals believe confession is a private matter between the person and God. The word here has the prefix which means "to confess out"—public confession. We are commanded to confess out "to one another." The present tense, describes continuous activity: "continually make a habit of confessing to one another." While confession to each other has no forgiving power, it certainly has significance.

We are called to confess our "trespasses" to one another. This means more than merely admitting our petty faults. The word here is the most common word for sin and means "missing the mark" (Rom. 3:23). The sins we are to confess are the specific things that grieve the heart of God. The blanket phrase "Lord, forgive us of our sins" is both trite and glib. God does not give out blanket amnesty, but forgives as we confess specifically.

Many people believe that if they have confessed to God, they need not confess to others. Yet some sins must be confessed to the one offended if the situation is to be effectively resolved. Sin strains the relationship with God and with the one(s) against whom the sin has been committed. To remove the strains, you must confess in both directions. The circle of the sin should be the circle of the confession. Thus, not all sins need to be confessed before the entire church—only the ones which affect the church.

Confession is not a substitute for repentance. Children are often guilty of quickly saying "I'm sorry!" in order to avoid the consequences. They are sorry but not repentant.

When Samuel confronted Saul after Saul's disobedience in failing to follow God's command to destroy the Amalekites, Saul insisted that he had obeyed the Lord. Samuel pressed him. Saul blamed his sin on the people. Samuel persisted. Finally Saul cried out, "I have sinned" (1 Sam. 15:24). Yet Saul was only trying to avoid the loss of his kingship. He was not repentant. The deception worked for him, so throughout the remainder of his reign, he voiced apparently sincere confessions while actually continuing his rebellion against God.

WHY CONFESS?

There are obvious benefits to confession. The process allows us to experience God's forgiveness. God forgave us for all sin—past, present, and future—on the cross (Col. 2:13-14), but we must confess and experience it personally. Sin thrives in private places. Bringing it into the open weakens its power over us—"so that you may be healed." Confession helps to create a healthy environment for the church. If we are "members of one another," we should "confess to one another" so that "we may be healed."

There are some practical suggestions for personal confession:

- Be sensitive in your timing—look for minimal interruption, and unrushed circumstances, with no distractions.
- Be selective in your wording. Avoid language of pride. You are admitting failure, not accusing them of something. If the other person is guilty, let the Holy Spirit convict them.
- Consider involving a third party, someone whose confidence you both can trust. Select one who can offer biblical counsel.
- Be specific in naming your sin, and accept full responsibility. Avoid vague terminology.
- Do not confess in stages, or the other person may begin to wonder if you are still holding something back.
- Give the other person time to deal with your confession. Don't expect an immediate response. They don't owe you forgiveness just because you confessed.

In his book *Your God is Too Safe*, Mark Buchanan recalls how, in the early 1990s former President George Bush once became suddenly, and violently ill at a state dinner in Japan. The media caught it all—the retching of the President, the revulsion of the Japanese Prime Minister, and the panic of the bodyguards who scrambled and rushed about as everyone else reacted in disgust.

We often feel that way about public confession—one person grovels and retches from deep within, revealing the revolting things on the inside that the Spirit insisted be shared, while everyone else watches in disgust. But consider the consequences should we have refused to obey—spiritual regression (Prov. 28:13); spiritual osteoporosis (Ps. 32:3); unanswered prayer; unhealed sickness (Jas. 5:16); phony fellowship (1 John 1:8).

Whatever shame and revulsion we might experience as we publicly confess under the Holy Spirit pales in comparison to the blessings received when we are obedient.

Pray that we would confess to one another.

Confess your trespasses to one another, and pray one for another, that you may be healed. The effective, fervent prayer of a righteous man avails much.

Jas. 5:16

praying for one another

1. Pray that God would reveal the hidden sins that have accrued in your life and soul, and confess them to Him.

2. Pray that God will humble you and your church enough to "come clean" with each other. Remember, God gives grace to the humble.

3. Pray that God will reveal to you those to whom you need to confess certain faults.

4. Pray that a spirit of brokenness over our sin will permeate our churches.

If we are to take in strangers and to care for and love them, how much more should we do towards the household of faith!

All believers have hospitality as a responsibility. Some will practice hospitality naturally, others with discipline and commitment.

PRAY THAT WE WOULD BE HOSPITABLE TO ONE ANOTHER
1 Peter 4:9

A MATTER OF PRIVILEGE

Peter has just encouraged his readers to "have fervent love for one another" (1 Pet. 4:8). Then he names one practical way of doing this, being "hospitable to one another." "Hospitality" literally means being friendly to strangers with "acts of kindness." This practice does not refer to social entertainment, but rather to lodging and meals.

We are to extend hospitality "without grudging," with cheerfulness—not because we have to, but because we are privileged to do so.

Duke University researchers did a study on "peace of mind." They found the factor that contributes most to emotional and mental instability was the nursing of a grudge.

This epistle was addressed to people scattered throughout different provinces offering numerous opportunities for showing hospitality. Without hospitality, the early church could not have existed, much less expanded. Traveling missionaries had no other place to stay than in homes (Heb. 13:2; Acts 10:6; 21:16). The inns that did exist were expensive, filthy, and often marked by immorality. For two hundred years, there were no church buildings; thus believers had to meet in homes (Rom. 16:5; 1 Cor. 16:19; Philippians 3).

Repeatedly in the Old Testament, the people of God are adjured to look after and take care of strangers. God "loves the stranger, giving him food and clothing" (Deut. 10:18). God has a special affinity for aliens and strangers, perhaps in anticipation of His coming to His own people, which resulted in being cast off and rejected. Clearly, in Christ, God knows what it is like to be in strange surroundings without a welcome. "He came to His own, and His own did not receive Him" (John 1:11).

God also commands His people to take in strangers because they, too, were once strangers and aliens in Egypt. They were not only to care for the stranger, but also to love him (Deut. 10:19). If we are to take in strangers and to care for and love them, how much more should we do towards the household of faith!

A MATTER OF RECOGNITION

One is reminded of Edwin Markham's poem, "How the Great Guest Came." Conrad, the old cobbler, dreamed one night that the Master Himself was coming to his humble abode to be his divine guest. When dawn came, he arose and decorated his little shop with bright flowers and waited excitedly. When the Master arrived, he would wash His feet and kiss His nail-scarred hands.

But the Master did not come. A beggar knocked, and Conrad gave him a pair of shoes. During the afternoon an old woman passed by, bowed down with the burden of a heavy load. He lifted the load and refreshed her with food. Then, just before nightfall, a little child came by, eyes wet with tears having lost the way home. In pity Conrad led the child back to the mother. But the divine Guest never came.

> Then soft in the silence a Voice he heard:
> 'Lift up your heart, for I kept my word.
> Three times I came to you friendly door;
> Three times my shadow was on your floor.
> I was the beggar with bruised feet;
> I was the woman you gave to eat;
> I was the child in the homeless street!'

As our Lord Himself has said, "Inasmuch as you did it to one of the least of these My brethren, you did it to Me" (Matt. 25:40).

Some believers have hospitality as a spiritual gift (1 Pet. 4:7-11; Rom. 12:13; 16:23; Acts 16:14-15; Heb. 13:1-2). All believers have hospitality as a responsibility. Some will practice hospitality naturally, others with discipline and commitment.

There are heroes of hospitality in Scripture who were especially used by God in the exercising of this gift. In the Old Testament, the Shunammite woman and her husband, built a room for the prophet Elisha to use as he frequently passed through their town.

In the New Testament, Jesus frequented the Bethany home of Mary, Martha, and Lazarus.

Just hours after the 9/11 attack on the World Trade Center, the Salvation Army set up a tent a block away from Ground Zero. There they offered bottled water, Gatorade, candy bars, medicated salve for noses to cover the smell of death, listening ears and caring hearts. For weeks the towers smoldered. The bottoms of the boots of the rescue workers were literally being burned through. As the workers came to the tent for a drink, the believers would remove the workers' boots and socks, wash and dry the tired feet, massage them, powder them, and put clean socks on them—as Jesus would have done.

Pray that we would be hospitable to one another.

Be hospitable to one another
without grumbling.

1 Pet. 4:9

praying for one another

1. Pray that your church would find a way to reach out regularly to new members, making them feel at home and assisting them in finding places of service.

2. Pray that God would lead you to the "unconnected" people in your church, and then invite them into your home.

3. Pray that God would give you someone to work with on your community's "Welcome Wagon." If there isn't a Welcome Wagon organization in your city perhaps you could start one.

4. Pray that God will lead you and others to entertain systematically every person in your Sunday school class this year.

Fellowship with the living God is the greatest companionship of all. And genuine fellowship with His saints comes next.

When we walk together in His light, strife gives way to peace; hatred yields to love; chaos evolves into order.

PRAY THAT WE WOULD HAVE FELLOWSHIP WITH ONE ANOTHER
1 John 1:7

WHERE THERE IS LIGHT THERE IS FELLOWSHIP

Gnosticism—the prevailing thought of the day—taught that some people became so spiritual, so knowledgeable, that it no longer mattered if they sinned. John is responding here to that idea. Numerous references to Gnosticism appear in early church history, from Clement of Alexandria to Irenaeus. John argued that if we say we have fellowship with Him, then we should walk like it. If we really walk in the light, we also have fellowship with one another.

Saying that we have this fellowship does not prove that we are walking in the light, but walking in the light proves that we have this fellowship. Where there is light, there is the potential for this fellowship.

Genuine, ongoing fellowship is impossible when people pretend to be something they are not, but when the light reveals all imperfections and expresses reality, then genuine fellowship can happen. First we accept one another, and then we have fellowship with one another.

This one anothering is not just about believers, it is about God and believers, since we walk with one another and walk with Him in the light.

What is the greatest thing in the world? Or in Socrates' terms, what is the "Highest Good"? Christians know it is not wealth or power or status or possessions.

The world values education, power, and riches. But God tells us in Jeremiah 9:23-24, "Let not the wise man glory in his wisdom. Let not the mighty man glory in his might, nor let the rich man glory in his riches; but let him who glories glory in this, that he understands and knows Me."

At Wedgwood Baptist Church, our motto is, "To know Christ and to make Him known." We often sing "Knowing You, Jesus, knowing You. There is no greater thing."

Fellowship with the living God is the greatest companionship of all. And genuine fellowship with His saints comes next. Fellowship is far more than cookies and Kool-Aid in the fellowship hall. Genuine, biblical fellowship is an open involvement in one another's lives. In order for this to occur, we must be open and transparent.

Just as secret sin and hypocrisy destroy our fellowship with God, so also sin and hypocrisy make genuine fellowship impossible within the body.

Transparency occurs when we trust each other enough to reveal our true selves, warts and all. This can only happen in a safe environment where one can reveal sin and needs, without being condemned or castigated.

Have we allowed our churches to become museums for plaster saints rather than hospitals for wounded folks? One can never be healed if he refuses to admit his sickness.

WHERE WE ARE "ONE ANOTHERING" WE HAVE FELLOWSHIP

Our leaders must lead the way. If they would climb down off their pedestals and openly share their weaknesses, needs, and struggles, perhaps others would follow suit. But if church is a place where one must be perfect, or nearly so, in order to be accepted, we will always have a toxic faith that shatters under the slightest pressure.

Genuine fellowship involves "weeping with those who weep, and rejoicing with those who rejoice." It involves honoring, being patient, accepting, burden-bearing, serving—in fact, all of the "one anothers" lead to genuine fellowship within the body.

And when we live in open fellowship with God's children, His body, our fellowship with Him grows deeper and sweeter.

Thus fellowship with one another grows out of the fellowship we have with God. Sin disrupts our fellowship, alienating us from each other. True fellowship can only be restored when all parties come together into God's light. When we walk together in His light, strife gives way to peace; hatred yields to love; chaos evolves into order.

Wedgwood Baptist Church in Fort Worth, Texas, has some of the greatest fellowship of any church. It intensified after we began to walk out of a common darkness—into a common light. You don't have to experience a tragic shooting in your church to produce great fellowship. Churches and individuals go through various tests of fellowship—the dark periods in life. You can overcome. If you will walk together through and out of this common darkness, toward a common light and continue to walk in the light, you can have genuine fellowship with one another.

Pray that we would have fellowship with one another.

If we walk in the light
as He is in the light,
we have fellowship
with one another. . . .

1 John 1:7

praying for one another

1. Pray that God will give you several close friends within your church with whom you can be completely open and honest.

2. Pray for your pastor and church leaders that they would be able to model openness and transparency for your congregation.

3. Pray that God will grow a prayer ministry in your church where real needs can be expressed and for which they may be interceded.

4. Pray that God will give leadership in leading your congregation in appropriate openness that will foster healing and fellowship.

The ministry of one anothering is open to all believers. It doesn't require a platform, a pulpit, a building, a budget, or board approval.

HUGGING ONE ANOTHER THROUGH PRAYER

One fall, a young woman was traveling alone up the rutted and rugged highway from Alberta to the Yukon. She didn't know that you don't travel to Whitehorse alone in a rundown Honda Civic, nevertheless she set off where only four-wheel drive vehicles normally venture. The first evening she found a room in the mountains near a summit and asked for a 5:00 a.m. wake-up call so she could get an early start. She couldn't understand why the clerk looked surprised at that request, but as she awoke to early morning fog shrouding the mountaintops, she understood. Not wanting to look foolish, she got up and went to breakfast. Two truckers invited her to join them, and since the place was so small, she felt obliged. "Where are you headed?" one of the truckers asked.

"Whitehorse," was the reply.

"In that little Civic? No way! This pass is dangerous in weather like this," exclaimed one of the truck drivers.

"Well, I'm determined to try," was the gutsy, if not very informed response.

"Then I guess we're just going to have to hug you," the trucker suggested.

The shocked young lady drew back. "There's no way I'm going to let you touch me!"

"Not like *that!*" the truckers chuckled. "We'll put one truck in front of you and one in the rear. In that way, we'll get you through the mountains."

All that foggy morning, the lady in the little car followed the two red dots in front of her and had the reassurance of a big escort behind as they made their way safely through the mountains.

Truck drivers hugging a little car occupied by a brave young woman is not unlike believers praying other believers through the challenges of life. Caught in the fog of our dangerous passage through life, we need to be "hugged" by one another. With fellow Christians who know the way and can safely lead us, and with others behind, gently encouraging us along, we too can pass safely.

The ministry of one anothering is open to all believers. It doesn't require a platform, a pulpit, a building, a budget, or board approval. You can begin today—with no training and no experience, and you don't have to quit your other job to do this. You can't be voted into this ministry, and you can't be voted out. So, get to hugging one another through prayer. Bill and Gloria Gaither may have said it best:

"I'm so glad I'm a part of the family of God. . . ."

and you know the rest of the story!

*Standing by the memorial
to the seven who lost their
lives in the September 15,
1999 shooting at Wedgwood
Baptist Church are authors
Al Meredith and Dan Crawford.*

Dr. Albert R. Meredith, a native of Michigan, has been the Senior Pastor at Wedgwood for seventeen years, having previously served as Professor of History at Anderson College in Anderson, South Carolina, and as pastor of the First Baptist Church in Elberton, Georgia.

Dr. Dan R. Crawford, a member of Wedgwood, is Professor of Evangelism & Missions and occupant of the Chair of Prayer at nearby Southwestern Baptist Theological Seminary. He is the author of the book on the Wedgwood shootings, *Night of Tragedy Dawning of Light* (Colorado Springs: Shaw Publishers, 2000).

These two have teamed up to write this book on praying for one another by using the thirty-one New Testament uses of the Greek word *allelon*—often translated *one another* in English.